HEALTHY, HAPPY BABY

The essential guide to raising
a toxin-free baby

PAT THOMAS

This edition first published 2008 by Rodale
an imprint of Pan Macmillan Ltd
Pan Macmillan, 20 New Wharf Road, London N1 9RR
Basingstoke and Oxford
Associated companies throughout the world
www.panmacmillan.com

ISBN 978-1-9057-44-24-4

Copyright © 2008 Pat Thomas

The right of Pat Thomas to be identified as the author of this work has been asserted in
accordance with the Copyright, Design and Patents Act of 1988.

Portions of the text in this book were published previously in *What's In This Stuff?* by Pat
Thomas, also published by Rodale.

1 3 5 7 9 8 6 4 2

A CIP catalogue record for this book is available from the British Library.

Printed and bound in the UK by CPI Mackays, Chatham ME5 8TD

This book is intended as a reference volume only, not as a medical manual. The information
given here is designed to help you make informed decisions about your health. It is not
intended as a substitute for any treatment that you may have been prescribed by your doctor.
If you suspect you have a medical problem, we urge you to seek competent medical help.
Mention of specific companies, organizations or authorities in this book does not imply
endorsement of the publisher, nor does mention of specific companies, organizations or
authorities in the book imply that they endorse the book.
Addresses, websites and telephone numbers given in this book were correct at the time of
going to press.

Visit *www.panmacmillan.com* to read more about all our books and to buy them. You will also
find features, author interviews and news of any author events, and you can sign up for e-
newsletters so that you're always first to hear about our new releases.

We inspire and enable people to improve their lives and the world around them

Acknowledgements

Writing a book requires the support of family, friends and colleagues, all of whom are prepared to tolerate various sorts of absences – physical, mental and emotional. Love and thanks to the wonderful 'constants' in my galaxy of stars: my son Alex, my agent Laura Longrigg, and my dear friends and colleagues at the *Ecologist* and to the hardest working Bull in show business. Gratitude also to Liz Gough and all at Pan Macmillan for support and a guiding hand along the way.

Other Rodale books by Pat Thomas

What's In This Stuff?
Skin Deep

Contents

Introduction

Protecting Our Children

We live in a toxic world, and pregnancy is often the first time women and their partners begin to become aware of this: pesticides in our food, pollution on the street, chemicals in the workplace or at home. Once you have a new life growing inside of you it is not uncommon to begin taking what can sometimes be an overwhelming inventory of all the things that could harm it – and to want to do all you can to protect that life.

Knowing where to start can seem daunting. The aim of this book is to provide a jumping-off point. The information here can help you weigh up your options in an à la carte way, to help you lead a healthier lifestyle and create a safer home environment so you feel more empowered to make decisions during pregnancy and beyond.

The steps you take to protect your children need not be complicated, however, and often adequate nutrition combined with a low-toxic lifestyle is the most effective approach, and can be less expensive and less complicated than many parents might imagine. Indeed, while there are lots of things that you will need to buy for a new baby – and you will soon see that there are lots of green alternatives to conventional baby products – in the end, protecting your baby is not so much about *buying* green so much as *being* green, and understanding why that is such an important choice.

Human babies are unlike any other young animals in that they are born completely helpless and with many of their bodily functions such as their digestion and immune systems still not functioning optimally. This is why extra care is needed, for instance in how you choose to feed, or in being alert for potential sources of exposure to toxic chemicals and fumes.

Babies indulge in lots of hand-to-mouth activity, transferring foreign substances into their bodies. Young children are also more likely to have close encounters with the pesticides on lawns and toxins in carpets, since they spend a lot of time playing or crawling on the ground.

There are other less obvious threats to health as well. The average newborn, owing to a faster metabolism and immature immune and detoxification systems, may:

- Spend the first year of life in a new crib with a mattress that's been treated with pesticides and fire-retardant chemicals. The foam inside the mattress can give off toxic formaldehyde gas, and the dyes used in sheets and covers are usually carcinogenic (cancer-causing). The typical crib headboard or bed frame is constructed from particleboard – pressed wood shavings glued together with a urea-formaldehyde resin that also gives off toxic gases.
- Wear disposable nappies made of bleached paper which emits a slow, steady dose of carcinogenic dioxins. They also contain a 'chemical sponge' which emits hormone-disrupting chemicals.
- Get nourishment from a plastic bottle that gives off phthalates (plasticisers) in such quantity that they can be measured in the bloodstream. If that were not enough, the formulas that many babies drink are deficient in the correct fatty acids necessary to promote optimum brain development.
- In the absence of a reassuring breast, be encouraged to suck on teethers and toys made of similarly toxic plastics.
- Travel in a brand-new moulded plastic baby carrier and car seat which has been treated with toxic flame retardant and which off-gasses toluene and more plasticisers.

The average parent may simply shrug and reason that none of these things on their own could possibly expose their child to enough toxins to cause illness. In a sense this is correct. Individually these things may not cause harm. But collectively they create a powerful combination of harmful chemicals from which a baby has no escape.

Chemical overload

It is impossible to say how many different and potentially harmful chemicals we each carry in our bodies. This is because beyond chemicals that are added to food or used as drugs, there is no requirement for manufacturers to disclose how their chemicals are used or keep track of the routes through which people are exposed. Nor are they required to understand the fate of their chemicals in the environment, measure concentrations of their products in the environment or in people, or develop and share methods of analysis that would allow other scientists to gather this kind of information independently.

In the largest study of chemical exposure ever conducted on human beings, the US Centers for Disease Control and Prevention (CDC) showed that that most American children and adults were carrying in their bodies more than 100 substances that aren't supposed to be there, including pesticides and the toxic compounds used in everyday consumer products, many of them linked to potential health threats.

Many toxicologists and environmental scientists reviewing the report expressed grave concern that in studies of animals, and in some cases, of people, most of these compounds could affect the brain, hormone balance, reproductive system or the immune system, or that they were linked to cancer.

The report documented the fact that many children were carrying much higher levels of these chemicals than adults, including some synthetic chemical compounds called pyrethroids, which are in virtually every household pesticide; and phthalates, the plasticisers found in nail polish and other beauty products as well as in soft plastics.

Throughout the world, the phenomenon of polluted people is becoming more commonplace. In order to understand more about the amounts and types of toxins we carry, the environmental group, the World Wildlife Fund (WWF), conducted a series of blood tests on people from all walks of life in the UK. In 2003 they tested the blood of individuals across the country and found an average of 27 chemicals in the blood of every one. These included long-banned chemicals such as the organochlorine pesticide DDT and PCBs from old electrical equipment and building materials, as well as common chemicals found in everyday materials such as paints, glues, toys, electrical goods, furniture, carpets and clothes.

The following year they tested the blood of environment ministers from 13 European Union countries and found a total of 55 different chemicals in the ministers' blood. The lowest number of chemicals found in any one minister's body was 33; the highest was 43, and these chemicals were the pollutants commonly found in sofas, pizza boxes and pesticides.

If your total toxic load is high, the likelihood of the body breaking down under the weight of it becomes higher

In 2005, the WWF tested the blood of a handful of British celebrities and found, on average, 24 chemicals in each one. The chemicals they found included DDT and PCBs; brominated flame retardants found in furniture and electrical equipment; phthalates found in perfumes, cosmetics and flexible plastics; perfluorinated chemicals found in the Teflon used in non-stick pans and the Scotchguard used in stain-proofing treatments.

The same year, a Canada-wide study that tested for a broad range of chemicals in average Canadians, found toxic chemicals, such as DDT, PCBs, stain repellents, flame retardants, mercury and lead, in every person sampled.

What these unique surveys show is that no matter where you live or what you do, you are unlikely to be able to avoid the kinds of chemical exposure that can lead to chemical overload.

How much is too much?
Many of the chemicals we are exposed to each day are 'persistent' – that is instead of breaking down they remain intact – and dangerous – in the environment and in our bodies for years, even decades. What this means is that small regular doses can and do increase our toxic load and build up to health harming levels over time.

Scientists refer to the accumulation of such chemicals as an individual's 'body burden' or 'total body load' – the consequence of lifelong exposure to industrial chemicals that are used in thousands of consumer products and linger as contaminants in our air, water, food and soil.

These chemicals come from household products like detergents, cosmetics, fabric treatments and paints as well as upholstery, computers, plastics and TVs. They accumulate in fat, blood and organs, or are passed through the body in breast milk, urine, faeces, sweat, semen, hair and nails. Over time, if the total body load is high, the likelihood of the body breaking down under the weight of it becomes higher.

THE COCKTAIL EFFECT

When two or more toxic or potentially toxic chemicals are combined together either in a product or in the human body, they can produce a toxic effect much greater than could be predicted by the sum of their individual effects. This phenomenon, known as the 'cocktail effect', is not widely reported in the press so many parents remain unaware of the dangers of these synergistic effects of exposure to more than one chemical at a time.

Most research into the cocktail effect has so far centred on hormone-disrupting chemicals present in the environment either as dietary supplements or as pollutants. For instance, British research published in 2002 found that combinations of minute levels of eleven environmental oestrogens including genistein (one of the main oestrogens in soya), resorcinol monobenzoate (a protective coating commonly found on plastic items such as computer mice, sunglasses, hearing aids and ballpoint pens), phenyl salicylate (a sunscreen agent) and bisphenol A (commonly found in baby bottles and other hard plastics) had more than doubled the oestrogenic effect on living cells that could have otherwise been predicted. Oestrogen in levels higher than those naturally produced by the body can trigger reproductive abnormalities and, in the longer term, cause cancer.

The 'low-dose effect' suggests that even small doses of certain chemicals can have big repercussions on health in both the short and long term. What constitutes a 'low dose' is not always clear, though it's generally defined as a dose much smaller than would normally be expected to have an effect.

The idea that small doses can have big effects is beginning to receive a great deal of serious attention from scientists throughout the world, some of whom have found that chemicals in traces as dilute as a few parts per trillion have profound biological effects. Worryingly, these low-dose effects can often be seen at levels well below those that have been deemed safe by regulatory authorities. This phenomenon has been particularly well researched in the field of hormone disruption, where even minute quantities of different oestrogen mimics present in the environment can produce an effect on the body that is many times greater than would be expected. For instance:

- **Phthalates**. Extremely low levels of phthalates, the oestrogen-like chemicals found in soft toys, building materials, drug capsules, cosmetics and perfumes, have been linked to sperm damage in men and genital changes, asthma and allergies in children.
- *Bisphenol A*. Minuscule doses of *bisphenol A*, which is used in polycarbonate plastic baby bottles and in resins that line food cans and in dental sealants, have been found to cause health effects at levels 2,500 times lower than the US Environmental Protection Agency's (EPA) 'lowest observed effect' dose. Exposure to low levels of this chemical has been reported to alter brain structure, neurochemistry, behaviour, reproduction and immune response in animals.

There are several reasons why low doses can be dangerous. One is that some people are simply more sensitive than others. Allergy specialists understand this problem well. When a person becomes sensitised to an allergen – for example peanuts or cat hair – exposure to even the tiniest amounts can set off a dramatic reaction. In chemically sensitive individuals exposure to even small amounts of certain chemicals may be all that is required to trigger a reaction.

The timing of an exposure is also influential. For instance, with many chemicals a low dose to a baby in the womb or during childhood can produce potentially much more serious toxic effects than similar exposures during adulthood. Good examples of this can be seen with the heavy metals lead and mercury, where low dose exposures in utero and during infancy cause permanent brain and nervous system damage, while the same doses appear to cause no observable effects in adults. Similar problems have been found with exposure to certain pesticides in babies and infants.

Children are vulnerable

In a polluted world, women, particularly pregnant women, and children are among those who are at most risk. Both tend to be smaller and so are exposed to more toxins per pound of body weight; women have naturally more body fat than men any way. Toxins are stored in body fat and can be released during pregnancy and breastfeeding when the body is using up its stores of energy more rapidly. Babies and young children also have less mature immune systems that cannot easily repair damage from toxins.

A child's response to toxic exposures is often very different from that of adults. Good examples of this are the paradoxical responses to phenobarbital and methylphenidate (Ritalin) in children compared to adults. Phenobarbital acts like a sedative in adults, but produces hyperactivity in children; Ritalin, a cocaine-like drug, is used as an anti-hyperactivity drug in children, but has a stimulant effect in adults.

There are many reasons for this paradoxical response. But perhaps the most influential is that in the womb and in the first two years after birth, children undergo extraordinary cell growth in every part of their bodies, from brain neurons to immune cells, so there are more opportunities for toxic compounds to disrupt the cells.

During childhood, different systems and organs develop at different rates and in different phases. Growing tissue is also much more sensitive to toxic exposures than other tissue and remains sensitive right into the teenage years. Indeed, studies of exposure to cigarette smoke have shown that the risk of dying of breast cancer is greater for those who started smoking before age 16 than for those who started smoking after age 20.

In addition to growing and developing, children differ from adults in a number of other ways that can increase their susceptibility to toxins.

For example:

- Their body systems have a less-developed ability to break down toxins; children's bodies may also have less capacity to repair damage as well.
- They eat, drink and breathe in more for their weight than adults, which means they take in more toxins per kilogram of body weight than adults: even at rest, an infant will be breathing in twice the volume of air as an adult.
- They crawl around on the floor near dust and other potentially toxic particles.
- They are more likely to put things in their mouths and eat things that they shouldn't.

In addition, the developing foetus is extremely sensitive to toxic chemicals. This is because the developing body is acutely sensitive to the signals and complex interactions of hormones. Disruption of these signals and interactions can disrupt the body's normal development.

Many studies show that hypertension, coronary heart disease, thyroid dysfunction, cancer, diabetes, asthma, arthritis and even Alzheimer's disease – things which can't be picked up on a prenatal scan – are all programmed into a baby while still in the womb. What determines the programming is maternal nutrition and exposure to environmental toxins before and after birth.

While it may appear that despite all this our children are being born alive and well, a closer look at infant health trends says otherwise.

Today, it is estimated that every year, each of us eats 6.3kg (14lb) of preservatives and additives, breathes 1g of heavy metals and has 4.5l (1 gallon) of pesticides and herbicides sprayed on our fruit and vegetables. And while it may appear that in spite of all this our children are unaffected, a closer look at infant health trends says otherwise.

Population studies tell us that the rate of birth defects has increased in recent years. In the US one report showed that 18 of the 20 most common birth defects were on the rise – some by as much as 1,700 per cent. Reports from the UK show a similar trend. In the West, some problems, such as undescended testicles, have become so much more common that they are no longer recorded as malformations.

Furthermore, more subtle trends have emerged. Among children, rates of asthma and other respiratory problems are on the rise, as are skin conditions, learning and behavioural difficulties and serious conditions such as Attention Deficit Hyperactivity Disorder (ADHD). Childhood cancers are also on the rise.

The worst effects of environmental poisons on children can clearly be seen in the increasing rate of childhood cancers – now the second biggest killer of children. Cancer is, of course, a multifactoral disease – many things can trigger it. But while scientists continue to focus their research on the genetic links to childhood cancer, important environmental triggers – in the form of mercury-containing vaccines, pesticides, food additives, household-chemical exposures and electromagnetic radiation – are being ignored.

It is estimated that every year, each of us eats 6.3kg of preservatives and additives, and has 4.5l of pesticides and herbicides sprayed on our fruit and vegetables

Science has shown us undeniably that good health begins before birth and that the best way to ensure a healthy baby is for parents to take seriously the responsibility for their own health and environment as early as possible – ideally before conception, but if that is not possible then preferably before birth.

In order to confirm whether or not a baby in the womb is all right we now use a whole range of antenatal procedures including ultrasound, blood tests and foetal heart monitors. But while these may be superficially reassuring, they can only tell you if something is wrong. None can help you grow a healthier baby. Exposure to environmental poisons are as crucial to the baby's future health and wellbeing as the mother's nutritional status.

What becomes clear from this information is that doing what you can to reduce your exposure to environmental toxins today has to be part of any plan for a healthy baby. A good diet on its own isn't enough because many everyday toxins and pollutants can interfere with the way nutrients are used in your body. Lead, for example, can deplete the body of calcium and zinc – both crucial for mental and physical development. In turn, low levels of zinc are associated with many different types of congenital abnormalities, especially urogenital abnormalities in boys.

As the science continues to mount on the damaging effects in children from exposure to pollution and everyday environmental toxins, there are compelling reasons to take the information in this book on board – even if sometimes it seems a bit scary.

But don't let the information in this book panic you. Instead, let it 'lift the lid' on certain topics and challenge and inform your thoughts about how you are going to approach life as a parent. Given the increasingly polluted state of our environment, there has been a renewed interest by increasing numbers of parents in natural methods of ensuring a child's good health. My aim is to show that, for most prospective parents, making small changes, such as the switch to an organic, low-toxin lifestyle, is the most practical and most effective way forward to ensuring a healthy, happy baby.

Chapter 1

A Healthy Pregnancy

On its own, your body is supremely capable of creating the perfect environment for a healthy baby to grow in. But this doesn't mean that you have no conscious contribution to make. Many aspects of our modern lifestyle – for instance, stress, financial pressures, poor dietary habits, sedentary lifestyles and a polluted environment – seem to conspire to make your body's job more difficult.

You can help your pregnant body do its task well by protecting it from the onslaughts of modern life. Because mother and baby are a single unit, whatever you do to maintain your body's health will also benefit your baby. Good health practices before and during pregnancy can ease even the most uncomfortable symptoms of pregnancy as well as ensuring better long-term health for your child.

Although it is not often viewed in this way, pregnancy can be a surprisingly powerful time in a woman's life. That sense of empowerment is very important to help see you through the challenges of parenthood that lie ahead. Unfortunately, too many women experience it from a position of utter powerlessness, anxiety and frustration.

Too often we choose to associate pregnancy with illness and the need for medical care. We accept the negative images of pregnant women – sickly, easily confused, hormonally challenged – in much the same way that we choose to associate breastfeeding women with cows

– rather than more powerful and inspiring mammals such as lionesses, gazelles or even dolphins.

Conventional medical management of pregnancy and birth, with its seemingly endless conveyor belt of hospital appointments and tests can reinforce some widespread and deeply ingrained insecurities which women have about their bodies, heightening their sense of fear, bewilderment and helplessness rather than promoting skill, competence and confidence. It can also mask the single most important truth about pregnancy – healthy mothers make healthy babies.

Your nutritional needs

One of the most important aspects of a healthy pregnancy is adequate nutrition. For as long as we have been studying human health, it has been obvious that to a large extent, we are what we eat. A great deal of research has accumulated to show that what a mother eats while pregnant can have a truly dramatic effect not only on how her baby grows while inside her but also on the long-term health of that child.

There are now a wealth of studies to show that hypertension, coronary heart disease, thyroid dysfunction, diabetes and the propensity toward other autoimmune diseases and degenerative diseases such as Alzheimer's are all programmed into a baby while still in the womb. What determines the programming, to a large extent, is maternal nutrition during that time.

We also know that the miscarriage rate goes up in women who are not adequately nourished. While many things – for instance older motherhood, the health problems associated with being very overweight, a history of miscarriage and difficulty conceiving – can increase the risk of miscarriage, being underweight has a startlingly high influence on the chances of miscarriage. A 2006 study found that miscarriage was 72 per cent more likely in women who were underweight. In this study, a better diet and supplements helped improve the outlook for underweight women. It is ironic that we now have many drugs and methods for helping women who find it difficult to conceive, but we still ignore perhaps the simplest solution: change your diet, put on some weight and try again.

While many women assume that as long as they are getting a fairly good diet everything will be fine, this may not be the case. If the mother eats a moderately good diet the baby may be fine, but she could begin to feel increasingly tired, unwell and unable to cope. If the mother is on a poor diet, her health and that of her baby may rapidly begin to deteriorate.

A very poor or restrictive diet can quickly begin to have detrimental effects on the baby: chief among these is poor foetal growth. There is evidence to show that during famine conditions, the average birth weight can go down by as much as 550g (1lb 3oz). In the affluent West it would be easy to argue that the term 'famine conditions' only applies to poor countries. Nevertheless, around a third of the babies born in the UK are born into families who are defined as 'poor'. Furthermore, dietary restriction, whether self-imposed out of a fear of getting 'fat' or medically directed, can have exactly the same effect, subjecting healthy women to the kind of famine-like conditions which can adversely affect their babies' growth.

Some women might wonder whether having a small baby is such a bad thing – surely it will make the birth easier? But the overwhelming evidence tells us that low-birth-weight babies are the ones who find labour the most distressing, who have the lowest health scores after birth, who are at greater risk of dying in the first six weeks of life and whose long-term physical and emotional health prospects are among the poorest.

A pregnant woman's heightened sense of taste and smell can make meals more interesting

If a mother has fears about growing a big baby or having a difficult birth, these must be addressed with rational information and the reassurance that a) women seldom make babies that are 'too big' to come out, and b) the size of your baby has very little to do with the kind of labour you will experience.

Although it is usual to scan babies regularly for birth defects, doctors often omit to tell mothers that under famine conditions the rate of birth defects also goes up.

For all these reasons, diet is arguably the most important aspect of maternal self-care and yet this is one thing which women rarely receive any coherent advice about. In fact, when women think of diet and pregnancy they usually think in terms of restriction. They think of what they're advised not to eat or drink – soft cheeses, shellfish, wine and beer – and what the doctor or midwife has told them they should cut back on – salt, coffee, tea, spices and even water. They think of food cravings and aversions. Or they focus on nutritional magic bullets like iron, folic acid and magnesium, instead of total nutrition.

Rarely do they think of what they can and should include in their diets or that food during pregnancy can become meaningful and enjoyable. It may never occur to them that a pregnant woman's heightened sense of taste and smell can make meals more interesting.

Not only does what you eat provide the building blocks for your baby's growth, it also provides, quite literally, a taste of the environment it will be born into. Several studies have shown that amniotic fluid becomes flavoured according to what the mother eats. In this way it is thought that babies become acclimatised to the food preferences of their culture.

We know that babies have a natural sweet tooth. In one study of babies who were growing poorly, the mother's amniotic fluid was sweetened with a sugar solution in an attempt to get the babies to drink more of it – and they did! Less appealingly, it has recently been discovered that babies can, in the same way, taste the tobacco that their mothers breathe in when they smoke cigarettes. Scientists now believe that the taste and the craving for tobacco is passed on from mother to infant in this way.

LIFTING THE LID

Observation of traditional cultures less steeped in junk food than ours shows that it only takes one generation of eating a typical Western diet – one high in fats, sugars and salt, and the type of 'empty' calories which do not provide any nutritional benefit, and low in fresh produce and complex carbohydrates – to begin to adversely affect their children's health.

But as important as nutrition is, we are also more than the sum total of what we eat. Outside influences such as the amount of stress we are under and the amount of pollution we are exposed to will also influence how well we assimilate and utilise nutrients. However, when you are pregnant your body will generally be using food more efficiently, so if your appetite is larger than before make sure you are eating with a purpose. Junk-food binges are as unwise as alcohol binges.

Common sense dictates that you should avoid refined and processed foods, in particular those that have a high sugar content since sugar has an immediate depressive effect on the immune system, leaving you vulnerable to illness. Fatty foods and those which list additives, preservatives, flavourings, aromas and stabilisers among their ingredients should all occupy only a small part of your diet, if they are part of it at all. It may also be wise to limit your consumption of red meat (if not in frequency, in portion size), replacing it in your diet with oily and/or deep-sea fish and poultry. Stimulants such as coffee, tea, cocoa and cola, all of which contain caffeine, should also be consumed in moderation, if at all.

Hunger, not calorie counting, is likely to be your best guide to appropriate eating during pregnancy. Nevertheless, certain guidelines do apply. In practical terms you should aim to have, daily, the following foods:

- 5 portions of wholegrain products (cereals, breads, rice, etc.)
- 2 servings of green vegetables
- 4 glasses of milk, or you can substitute yogurt or make a milkshake
- 3 pats of butter or 70ml (3tbsp) of unrefined vegetable oil (olive, sunflower, rapeseed)
- 1 citrus fruit or similarly high-vitamin C food such as berries, tomatoes, cauliflower, potato or sweet potato
- 2 extra servings of high-protein foods, particularly fish and poultry, but also eggs, cheese, nuts and pulses
- plenty of caffeine-free drinks such as water, herb teas and grain coffees. Fruit juices are fine too, but limit or dilute these because they can be high in sugar.

In addition, five times a week you should include:

- a yellow- or orange-coloured fruit or vegetable, for example cantaloupe, sweet potato, papaya, carrot, mango, orange, apricot or squash.
- an iron-rich food; traditionally offal such as kidney. Liver consumption should be restricted during pregnancy (see p. 128). However, owing to the toxins which commercially reared animals ingest, you should only have offal from organically raised animals. Otherwise, consider suitable alternatives such as beans, nuts, asparagus, small portions of red meat, molasses, oatmeal and dried peaches, apricots and prunes.

One final recommendation is that the closer a food is to its natural state, the more nutrients you will get out of it. Thus fresh is optimum, frozen is acceptable, canned is fine but only from time to time. Eating produce in its raw state is ideal, particularly in the warmer months. However, if you like your vegetables hot, remember to steam or cook them only very lightly to preserve their nutrients.

If you are prepared to eat seasonally, you can get very fresh, organically grown produce from a number of suppliers around the

EATING FOR TWO

Remember that a diet for pregnancy is not a diet for life and that the recommendations in this book are simply guidelines. They can, and should, be adjusted to suit your individual tastes and preferences. In fact, more than any prescribed eating plan, variety is the key to getting all the nutrients you need.

While you are pregnant, go ahead and eat for two but remember that eating for two doesn't refer to the *quantity* you are eating – but rather its *quality*. If you restrict anything at all, make sure it is fast food with empty calories. Try opting instead for nutrient-dense foods naturally rich in the full range of the essential nutrients we all need for optimum health.

country. Apart from having no harmful pesticides, this food will have been picked fresh and arrive with relative speed to your table. This is in complete contrast to the produce in the supermarket which can be stored for months before being put on display, a process which depletes it of essential nutrients.

Should I take vitamin supplements?

In a perfect world we would get all of our vitamins and minerals from our food. But despite our best efforts, many of us simply do not have diets that give us everything we need. Optimum nutrition is important throughout your life, but is especially important during pregnancy when you are quite literally eating for two.

The health status of the mother (indeed, of both parents) is directly related to the health status of her baby. Astonishingly, given the importance of nutrition during pregnancy, there are very few official recommendations for what supplements women should and should not be taking – if any at all – at this time. Apart from an increase in folate intake early in pregnancy and increased thiamine in late pregnancy, there is no official reference nutritional intake (RNI) for most vitamins and minerals to guide pregnant women. Indeed, the Committee on Medical Aspects of Food Policy (COMA) of the Department of Health believes that pregnancy places no additional mineral requirement on a woman's body.

British RNIs recommend hardly any substantial increases for pregnancy. To make matters more complex, recommendations for the nutrient intakes during pregnancy in the UK are markedly different from those in the US and different again in countries such as France.

Amazingly, very little research has been done to guide us as to what is the normal nutrient intake in pregnancy of healthy women. While it is true that many pregnant women ingest nutrients at lower than recommended levels for non-pregnant women, the danger of recommending vitamins during pregnancy is that it distracts women from other necessary actions that may well help them improve their overall nutrient status.

Pregnant women need to increase their calorie intake by about 300–500 calories per day (from the non-pregnant requirement of about 2,200 calories per day to the pregnant requirement of about 2,500 calories per day). This additional requirement is less important in the first trimester (the first 13 weeks of pregnancy) and most important in the last. However, many women are afraid to increase their food intake at this time for fear of 'getting fat'.

Eating adequate protein during pregnancy is essential for foetal and placental growth. Current recommendations for pregnant women call for a 10–16g (¼–½ oz) per day increase over non-pregnant requirements, which is at least 60g (2oz) of protein every day. This does not require you to eat huge amounts and you can always check your protein intake against the values on food labels. For example, a 100g (3½oz) portion of roast chicken contains around 25g (1oz) protein; 100g (3½oz) grilled cod steak contains around 20g (⅔oz); a 28g (1oz) piece of cheddar cheese contains around 7g (¼oz); 250ml (9fl oz) skimmed milk contains 8g (⅓oz); 1 tablespoon of peanut butter 4g (⅙oz); 250g (9oz) serving of baked beans 12g (⅖oz).

If a woman's general calorie and protein intake is increased sufficiently and is made up of good-quality food, she may well also increase her nutrient intake significantly.

A woman who gets the full range of essential vitamins and minerals (not just folate and iron) is helping to reduce her risk of giving birth to a child with birth defects. One reason for this is that adequate levels of nutrients have an important role to play in helping the body to rid itself of toxins and limit the damage which toxins can cause to body tissues and organs.

LIFTING THE LID

The folic acid supplements women are recommended to take during pregnancy are a synthetic form of the naturally occurring nutrient folate. Folate is a member of the B-vitamin family found in a wide variety of natural foods (see Appendix 1), so you may be able to consume the advised quantity of folic acid from your food, without having to resort to an artificially made substitute.

HOW MUCH IS ENOUGH?

During pregnancy and while you are breastfeeding, you will need more of most types of vitamins. According to Patrick Holford, founder of the Institute for Optimum Nutrition, the optimum levels for the essential nutrients during pregnancy are as follows:

Optimum vitamin levels

A 7500iu
D 400iu
E 400iu
C 2000mg
B1 25mg
B2 25mg
B3 50
B5 50mg
B6 50mg
B12 50ug/mcg
Folic acid 800ug/mcg
Biotin 200 mg

Optimum mineral levels

Calcium 1200mg
Phosphorous 1200mg
Magnesium 600mg
Iron 18mg
Zinc 20mg
Sodium 3000mg
Chromium 50ug/mcg
Potassium 5000mg
Manganese 5mg
Selenium 25mg
Iodine 175mg

In addition to a daily multivitamin, you should consider a daily supplement of essential fatty acids (EFAs) since these are necessary for the development of your baby's brain and nervous system, for optimum immune system function and to help the body break down toxins. Most diets are high in omega-6 fatty acids which are found in many day-to-day foods. However, many of us are deficient in omega-3 fatty acids. Aim to supplement with 1g of omega-3 EFAs per day. Fish oils are the traditional way to get these, but they can be contaminated with mercury. If you don't think it is worth the risk, source your omega-3 EFAs from linseed or flaxseed oil instead.

If a woman's diet is less than adequate, or if regular exposure to toxic chemicals at home or at work is a worry, taking a multivitamin supplement could be likened to taking out an insurance policy. However, it is worth taking a closer look at the small print to see if your multivitamin supplement is giving you the optimum levels of all the essential nutrients. If yours is lacking, you should consider altering your diet to include more foods rich in the missing nutrients (see Appendix 1).

Since each nutrient your body takes in works synergistically to protect your body, it is very important that if you are supplementing you should take a full range of nutrients as can be found in a good quality multivitamin and mineral supplement. See the box on page 11 for more information.

Balancing exercise and rest

Pregnancy places a great many demands on your body. When you are pregnant, your body will change in ways you may not even be aware of. For instance, your heart will eventually double in size and the amount of blood in your body will also double. When one study compared the heart health of pregnant women to non-pregnant women it found that the cardiovascular fitness of the pregnant women was greater, even though they took significantly less exercise. Just being pregnant, it seems, is enough to give you an all-over body workout.

Nevertheless, for healthy, well-nourished women (and subject to only a few restrictions), exercise, particularly in early pregnancy, has some real benefits. A regular exercise programme will help relieve some of the transient discomforts of pregnancy such as constipation, haemorrhoids and insomnia. It will improve muscle tone and endurance, both of which are needed during labour. Exercise improves circulation, and those who engage in regular exercise tend to have more stable blood pressure. In the later part of pregnancy, regular, gentle exercise may be of benefit to women who are told they have gestational diabetes since it will help the body use insulin more efficiently. The deep regular breathing which is part of many exercises will enrich your blood with oxygen and will be as good a practice for labour as any prescribed breathing practice you might learn about in an antenatal class.

For busy women, exercise often gets incorporated into daily activities, for instance, taking the stairs in early pregnancy instead of the lift, or walking to the shops or the post office instead of taking the car. This is as legitimate as any other form of exercise. However, some women genuinely enjoy the social aspect of prenatal fitness programmes – getting together with other women at various stages of pregnancy and being part of a supportive group. What's more, there are psychological benefits in taking part in exercise which is strictly a leisure pursuit and which doesn't involve mundane household chores and running errands for other people.

Which exercise?

Your best choices include walking, swimming, tennis, cross-country skiing, dancing, weight training, sailing, Pilates, yoga and Alexander technique. These last three choices are particularly appropriate since they will improve your flexibility (both physical and emotional). During labour, flexibility will be more helpful than strength.

BETTER FOR BABY TOO?

Almost anything which promotes good health in the mother will benefit the baby. Better circulation, in particular, will mean that the placenta is enriched with nourishing blood and the baby may well enjoy and benefit from the rhythmic rocking motion of some exercises. If the mother is combining exercise with meditation such as in yoga, the hormones released in her relaxed state will also 'relax' the baby.

But as with everything else in pregnancy, there can be a downside to engaging in very vigorous exercise, particularly in late pregnancy. Lengthy aerobic exercise at this stage may reassure the mother about her health and her body, but sometimes it does not benefit the baby. Muscles need blood to work and during vigorous exercise blood gets diverted away from non-active muscles to those which are working the hardest. Late in pregnancy, exercising too hard can draw essential blood away from the uterine muscle and this can impact on the baby's health, compromising foetal growth and increasing the risk of pre-term labour. Given this, the third trimester may be a time to consider other, less demanding forms of exercise such as walking, yoga and swimming.

A helpful hint for choosing an exercise is to think about how your body feels and choose according to your needs. For instance, if you feel that your increasing weight is making you less flexible and light on your feet, swimming and especially yoga can do you a world of good. If you feel lethargic in early pregnancy, getting your heart rate up with an aerobic exercise can help move things along.

Be aware, though, that some exercises can make things worse. For instance, plunging yourself into a cold swimming pool may wake you up – but if you are prone to leg cramps, it could bring them on.

In addition, consider the following guidelines:

- Generally speaking, pregnancy is not a good time to take up a new, vigorous sport – staying with the familiar may be more advisable.
- Your heart rate should remain at comfortable levels and be monitored to avoid getting overheated, dizzy or short of breath. For women who engage in aerobic exercise, avoiding large arm movements should ensure that your heart rate does not rise too rapidly.
- You may want to pay more attention than usual to body temperature. Your baby cannot control its own body temperature and relies on you to be its thermostat. Not overheating or becoming too cold are sensible precautions. Try to stay hydrated during exercise and sports activities to help keep your body temperature within normal range.
- Jarring movements may be more risky during pregnancy and you should take special care to protect your lower back which will come under increasing stress as your pregnancy progresses. Likewise, running and anything which places a high impact on the muscles and skeleton, as well as activities which involve being off balance or suddenly changing direction, should be avoided late in pregnancy.
- Avoid scuba diving. The oxygen is too rich for your baby's system and the increased pressure on the systems of both mother and baby may starve the baby of necessary oxygen.
- In early pregnancy, cycling may be beneficial but on today's roads it can be hazardous and stressful. A helmet won't protect the most precious and vulnerable part of your body. Also, as you get heavier, your centre of gravity will shift and you may not feel as stable on a bicycle as you once did.

- If you are participating in organised events make sure your teacher is experienced in working with pregnant women, whose needs are different. Specially dedicated classes are often best.

Finally, when the uterus experiences excessive stress it will start to contract. Some forms of exercise, particularly those where the woman is using her legs, may cause uterine contractions due to stress on the womb. These mostly harmless contractions can be hard to notice unless you are very tuned into your body.

However, a contraction, even a mild one, can be a sign that the exercise is too intense and needs to be halted. Like any other muscle, when the uterus contracts it feels hard. By placing your fingers just below your diaphragm, it is possible to palpate the uterus to contraction. An experienced midwife or doctor can help you learn what this type of mild contraction feels like so that you can recognise it in the course of your exercise regime.

Exercising your pelvic floor

Your pelvic floor muscles may not show, but the more toned they are the more efficient they will be at aiding your baby's passage into the world. Doing your pelvic floor exercises also means that you are less likely to suffer any prolonged physical problems in this part of your body after birth.

The pelvic floor isn't really a floor at all, but a complex structure of muscles which supports everything in the pelvic cavity including the uterus, bladder and rectum. The easiest way to identify your pelvic floor muscles, if you have not already done so, is to imagine you are interrupting a stream of urine. These muscles also contract spontaneously during sexual intercourse, intensifying pleasure for you and your partner. Awareness and control of your pelvic floor muscles is also helpful during labour since you will need to release them as your baby passes through the birth canal.

The muscles around the opening of your vagina and your anus can be contracted together or separately. To contract the muscles around the vagina, imagine that you need to urinate but must hold it in. The 'holding' involves a contraction of the pelvic floor muscles. Contracting the muscles around the anus involves the same kind of 'holding' action.

You should aim to do your pelvic floor exercises twice daily, in sets of 20 to 30. You can do them in bed first thing in the morning and last thing at night or, if you're really motivated, in the car or on the bus, or anywhere you feel inclined. At first, some women find this exercise difficult. They don't see the point or find that their muscles tire easily and they can't keep them contracted for very long. Some find that when they try to tighten these muscles they end up holding their breath and tightening other muscles in their shoulders, neck and arms instead. But as with all exercise, it gets easier to do with practice and you will find that you will be able to relax and eventually hold the contracted muscles for up to a count of ten.

Taking time to rest

Every period of exercise should be balanced by a period of rest. This does not necessarily mean sitting around doing nothing. Rest time can be used to meditate and actively reflect. Any hobby that totally absorbs you will also be restful, since it will take your mind off things and allow you to focus totally on a single task.

The effects of stress in pregnancy are well studied. High levels of stress are also linked to greater risk of miscarriage. Raised levels of stress hormones such as cortisol in pregnant women have been linked to higher incidences of mental and behavioural problems in their children. A study in 2007 found that cortisol, which reaches the baby via the amniotic fluid in the womb, could affect the development of the brains of foetuses, affecting their future social skills, language ability and memory. Some studies link high cortisol levels in pregnancy to children who themselves produce high levels of cortisol and have a decreased ability to handle stress as well as to an increased risk of developing ADHD.

Not unnaturally, some pregnant women find that the quiet times are the most difficult. Instead of relaxing their minds and communing with the baby, they find they are overcome with nagging fears and doubts. You may find yourself worrying about whether you can cope during labour, whether you will be a good mother, how much time you can afford to take off around the time of birth, whether you will be able to meet the demands of your new baby and what your partner's reaction to new parenthood will be.

All of these worries are normal and legitimate, but don't be deluded into thinking that if you just make a greater effort you will find some sort of rational answer to it all. Pregnancy is a process. It is a journey into the unknown. Apprehension about the unknown is natural and learning to deal with the unfamiliar is good practice for all the future unknowns which crop up once you become a parent.

If anxiety and worries come up when it's quiet or during meditation, don't be too hard on yourself. Acknowledge them briefly and then try to let them go. Switching off for half an hour will make no difference to solving the riddle of impending motherhood and you will emerge more refreshed for having done so. If your worries persist then it is generally a sign that you don't have enough information about whatever is on your mind. Perhaps you haven't allowed yourself to fully explore what's worrying you. Or it could be a signal to talk to someone and ask more questions.

If you are concerned about your baby, or have questions about your pregnancy and find that your midwife or doctor is too busy or does not provide satisfactory answers, go elsewhere. Several useful groups exist to help provide information and support to pregnant women. Groups like the Association for Improvements in the Maternity Services (AIMS) and The National Childbirth Trust (NCT) provide telephone support as well as producing a wide range of booklets and leaflets. See the Resources section for more details.

If your anxieties centre around you and your partner, now is the time to open the channels of communication. The insights gained in moments of calm and reflection can be a useful starting point. Share your feelings in the best way you can and encourage your partner to do the same. If you can take a weight off your shoulders in this way, it can sometimes feel as good as if you've had a long, long rest.

In an active world, it's easy to forget that there are other forms of 'cardiovascular activity' which are important. Making room in your heart for this new little person is a big job, one which can only be done in moments of reflection and calm (see also Chapter 6).

Testing, testing

It's fair to say that most women perceive antenatal screening as a good thing. They perceive it as an important part of their care and don't always think of less-invasive procedures such as blood tests or ultrasound

Testing doesn't make a healthy baby – healthy parents make a healthy baby

as 'tests' at all. Instead, they see them as a way of addressing any concerns they might have about their baby's health. There is absolutely nothing wrong with antenatal testing as long as it is used appropriately and consciously by women and their practitioners. Unfortunately, most testing is done with both practitioner and mother on auto-pilot.

In unravelling the question of appropriate testing, a good place to start is by asking why so many healthy pregnant women feel at risk.

There is no simple, single answer. On a cultural level, routine testing – whether it's the seemingly trivial ritual of weighing a woman or the more invasive amniocentesis – reinforces some powerful insecurities. Since women are rarely brought up to believe in the perfection of their bodies, pregnancy can be a time of great uncertainty. After all, how can the female body, so widely perceived as imperfect, dysfunctional and largely out of control, create a perfect baby?

Apart from our out of proportion and often baseless perceptions of risk, another reason for high levels of anxiety are the conditions under which many women are expected to make decisions about their care. Options are usually presented early on, in the unfamiliar and uncomfortable setting of a hospital or clinic. The woman may be suffering from morning sickness, or extreme tiredness (see Appendix 2 for natural ways to treat pregnancy 'symptoms'). She may be under pressure from family or friends, who may themselves have experienced pregnancy and birth as a negative event, or who are fearful of the process. They may be pushing her to take action, take tests, in fact do anything, to ease their own anxiety about the coming birth.

The combination of an unfamiliar environment, unfamiliar physical symptoms and pressure from her nearest and dearest may make a woman feel as if there must be something wrong with her or her baby. She may agree to tests which in another state, physically and mentally, she would not otherwise consider necessary.

Is this test really necessary?
Although women have the right to refuse any or all of these interventions at any time, why would they when everything they have

16

been told indicates that these things are safe and desirable? Furthermore, from a medical standpoint, these procedures are a necessary part of 'doing birth right'. Some women, it must be said, also equate the amount of 'stuff' done to them with good, responsible care and the acceptance of this 'stuff' with being a good, responsible parent.

In a perfect world, a woman's decision to choose or refuse a test, and everything that follows it, should be based on good information. She wouldn't just agree to routine tests; she would *decide* about them. Choose them, or refuse them according to your own needs.

As the list that follows shows, each one has merits and risks that should be weighed up carefully. Yet most women's knowledge about antenatal screening is still very limited. Sometimes this is because practitioners convey little information or present it in a way that is misleading. Many doctors have such great faith in antenatal testing that they believe that discussion of the pros and cons is a waste of their already limited time. Some believe that 'too much' information will only worry or confuse mothers. This assumption is not borne out by fact; recent studies have shown that offering women more information does not confuse them or increase anxiety.

When considering special tests such as ultrasound, Chorionic Villus Sampling (CVS) or amniocentesis, remember that a diagnosis is not the same as a cure. Once diagnosed there is often little that can be done to correct a problem apart from offering the mother a termination. If you are one of the 30 per cent or so of women who would not consider a termination on any grounds, then there is little point of you going through the battery of tests on offer antenatally.

Before you panic, or let anyone around you panic, consider what your real risk is. There are a few simple questions you should ask of your practitioner, and yourself, before agreeing to any antenatal test. They are:

- Does this test directly benefit my baby? If so, how?
- What are the documented risks of the test? To myself? To my baby?
- How conclusive is the result?
- Can the condition you are testing for be cured or corrected either now or when the baby is born?
- How does knowing about this condition early benefit my baby or me?
- Would the outcome be the same if I didn't have the test?

Making sense of tests

Urine
- **Test:** A non-invasive test using a specially coated dip-stick
- **When offered:** First and subsequent antenatal visits
- **Uses:** Can confirm pregnancy. A sample may also be analysed for evidence of infection and traces of protein which may indicate pre-eclampsia.
- **Possible risks:** None, but dip-stick tests are notoriously difficult to read accurately. Two different practitioners may see two different results. Ask for a second opinion if the test indicates something wrong.

Blood pressure
- **Test:** Non-invasive measurement of the flow of your blood as it enters and leaves your veins.
- **When offered:** First and subsequent antenatal visits
- **Uses:** Checks primarily for abnormally high blood pressure. The number on top – the diastolic pressure – is when the blood enters the vein. The number on the bottom – the systolic pressure – is when it leaves. The combination of the two measurements provides a snapshot of your circulatory health, at that moment in time.
- **Possible risks:** None, but blood pressure can vary from day to day and from hour to hour. Normal blood pressure during pregnancy is between 100/60 to 125/80. In labour it can go up to 140/90 without indicating a problem. Many things can influence the results such as how tired or stressed you are. When blood pressure only rises in the clinic, this is called 'white-coat hypertension'. If you suffer from this, you can ask to have your blood pressure taken at home where you feel more relaxed.

AFP/double/triple/triple-plus test
- **Test:** Blood test which requires the drawing of a small amount of blood
- **When offered:** Offered at first antenatal visit
- **Uses:** Tests for a limited range of disorders, primarily Down's syndrome and spina bifida. Standard AFP test looks for a single

'marker', or chemical, in the blood; the double test, two 'markers' and so on.

- **Possible risks:** Terribly inaccurate. Only detects 50 per cent of affected babies; only 10 per cent of those thought to be at risk of having an affected baby actually do. Results can be made more inaccurate if your pregnancy is more advanced than the doctor believes, if you smoke, if you had an early bleed, if you are black and if you are carrying a boy or twins. In retrospect, many women regret having this test since they then become pressured into having a second, more invasive test to confirm or deny the results of the first.

Ultrasound
- **Test:** High-frequency sound waves are bounced off the foetus. The echo returned to the main machine is interpreted as a picture.
- **When offered:** Standard scan is performed around 16–20 weeks. Some women are offered more throughout pregnancy.
- **Uses:** Looks for a range of abnormalities including Down's syndrome, spina bifida, neural tube defects, heart conditions and other abnormalities of the internal organs. At best, only picks up 80 per cent of a limited range of abnormalities.
- **Possible risks:** Despite its widespread use, ultrasound is a largely unproven technology that has been associated with the rise in learning difficulties among children. There is mounting evidence it alters brain function and may also damage soft tissue. It is linked with an increased risk of miscarriage in women prone to miscarriage. Repeated ultrasound scans are no better than a single scan in improving outcomes, so consider limiting your and your baby's exposure.

Foetal heart monitor
- **Test:** A form of ultrasound which is used to listen to the foetal heart
- **When offered:** Used every antenatal visit unless the mother requests less invasive monitoring such as a Pinard (foetal stethoscope) or regular stethoscope.
- **Uses:** Contrary to popular belief, this is not a microphone. It is a complex ultrasonic device which scans the baby in the womb and interprets what it finds in the form of a heartbeat.
- **Possible risks:** Risks are hard to assess and are perhaps best

examined as part of the mother's total ultrasound exposure. If you are uneasy about exposing your baby to ultrasound you should ask to hear your baby's heartbeat with a stethoscope, or have it monitored by a hand-held Pinard.

Nuchal scan
- **Test:** Early ultrasound scan
- **When offered:** Usually performed before 12 weeks
- **Uses:** Looks for a special fold of skin behind the neck. Thicker folds are thought to be an indication of Down's syndrome.
- **Possible risks:** No evaluation has been made of how safe early scans are for the growing foetus. Recent studies have concluded that the nuchal scan is no better at detecting abnormalities than the standard scan and may carry more risks for the developing baby.

Transvaginal scan
- **Test:** Ultrasound through the vagina
- **When offered:** Can be given any time
- **Uses:** A probe which bounces ultrasonic beams off the baby is inserted in the vagina. Because it is closer to the baby, doctors say they get a clearer picture.
- **Possible risks:** The amount of ultrasound your baby will receive will be many times greater since it will not have the advantage of being protected by your abdominal muscles and fat. This is an intimately invasive test which carries all the same risks of other forms of ultrasound, perhaps more, as well as the risk of infection from having a foreign object inserted into the vagina. Should not be used on women with placenta praevia or a cervical stitch.

Chorionic Villus Sampling (CVS)
- **Test:** Laboratory analysis of tissue removed from the developing placenta
- **When offered:** Performed between 16 and 20 weeks
- **Uses:** A needle is inserted in the womb via the abdomen. It is used to withdraw amniotic fluid, which will then be analysed over a period of several weeks. Used to detect Down's syndrome, spina bifida and neural tube defects. Results will also reveal the sex of the child.

- **Possible risks:** You will be removing a tiny part of the placenta – a risk which some mothers feel is too great. Babies who have had CVS have more breathing difficulties raising the issue of whether the test may create health problems rather than solve them. The risk of club foot also rises with CVS. This is a special test to be reserved for those at high risk of having a child with an abnormality.

Anmiocentesis
- **Test:** Laboratory analysis of fluid removed from the womb
- **When offered:** Should be performed between 16 and 20 weeks
- **Uses:** A needle is inserted into the womb either through the cervix or the abdomen. The aim is to remove a small part of the chorion – the cells which will eventually develop into the placenta. These cells are analysed for signs of abnormalities such as spina bifida and Down's syndrome. Results will also reveal the baby's sex.
- **Possible risks:** Must be used with ultrasound otherwise the risk of the needle puncturing the baby is many times increased. Women may experience spotting and cramping afterwards and older women have a greater risk of miscarriage from the procedure. May cause breathing difficulties in the baby. Not always conclusive; some lab cultures fail and then the test must be done again. Many women find amnio uncomfortable and scary. Best reserved for special situations.

Pelvic X-ray
- **Test:** X-ray of the pelvic bone structure
- **Usually offered:** Usually offered towards the end of pregnancy
- **Uses:** Used to assess the internal dimensions of a woman's pelvis to see whether there is enough room for the baby to come out. Occasionally used to confirm congenitally misshapen pelvis.
- **Possible risks:** Very inaccurate and now abandoned by many hospitals as a means of assessing the dimensions of a woman's pelvis. Chances are your baby is not too big to come out. The risk of exposing your baby to X-rays is well documented and includes an increased risk of childhood cancer.

Making sense of your maternity care options, and indeed your options for birth, is the first step towards being an active participant

– instead of just a passenger – on the journey of growing and birthing a healthy baby.

Whether you perceive antenatal tests as reassuring or invasive, the truth is that testing doesn't make a healthy baby – healthy parents make a healthy baby. The best way to ensure the wellbeing of your baby is to focus less on testing and more on diet, exercise and rest.

How to grow a healthy baby – Part I

Here is your simple checklist for giving your baby the best possible start in life (see Chapter 2 for Part II):

- **Change your lifestyle before you become pregnant** It's the best way to guarantee a healthy baby. As little as six months' of effort – improving nutrition and taking exercise – can make all the difference. Many parents might reason that this effort is nothing compared to the emotional, physical, mental and financial effort it can take to look after a child with disabilities.

- **Get fit, but be careful about dieting** Stringent dieting accompanied by fast weight loss immediately before or during pregnancy depletes your own stores of nutrients, increases the chance that your baby will have birth defects and raises its risk of longer-term problems such as anaemia, heart and lung problems. In addition, many environmental toxins and pollutants are stored in fat. When you lose weight quickly these are released into your system in large amounts.

   While there is some merit in the idea of losing toxic fat before you conceive and replacing this with 'clean' fat gained from an organic diet, this should not be attempted on your own. If you intend to diet before conceiving, make it part of a long-term health regime. Enlist the help of a qualified nutritionist who can work with you to strengthen your body, replace lost nutrients and help aid the detoxification process. Leave six months between major weight loss and conceiving to make sure your body is completely clear of toxins that may harm your baby's development.

- **Eat to your fill** This is not the time to go on a diet even if you were excessively overweight when you became pregnant. Opt instead to improve the quality of what you are eating. Many women find that once on a nutrient-dense, wholefood diet they are naturally more satisfied with smaller meals. You may find your weight stabilises when you eat like this without compromising the healthy of your baby.

- **Make protein-rich food your priority** Animal and vegetable protein are both acceptable as long as you get enough of it. Your diet should also include plenty of foods rich in vitamins A, B complex, C and the bioflavonoids, D and E. Essential minerals such as calcium, magnesium, manganese, zinc, iron, iodine and phosphorous are part of a healthy diet, as are the essential fatty acids found in oils, fish and seeds, such as nuts and soya.
- **Avoid refined and processed foods**, foods with lots of additives and in particular those which have a high sugar content.
- **Consider supplements**, but don't mega-dose. It would be nice to think that our bodies could get all the nutrients they need from their diets, but this is just not possible. As our world becomes more and more polluted it is even more important to take a daily multivitamin and mineral supplement, since a well-nourished body is better able to cope with environmental insults. Listen to advice about supplements from your doctor or midwife.
- **Wash all fruits and vegetables thoroughly** Try to include at least some organic food in your diet. Since organic food is grown without pesticides it may include microscopic 'pests', so make sure you wash all this produce thoroughly too.
- **Season your food to taste** Salt, for instance, is necessary for the proper functioning of our nerves and muscles. During pregnancy, cutting out salt entirely may be unwise since pregnant women generally sweat more and so lose more salt through their skin.
- **Follow a stress-relief programme** Stress depletes the body of essential nutrients – especially B-vitamins. Mothers who are under lots of stress tend to have babies who are smaller and less active in the womb. Stress also depresses your immune system – this means that you are less able to fight off the effects of toxins which are ingested and inhaled.

In a recent US study, women who had strenuous jobs, such as those which require repetitive tasks, had a higher rate of problems including pre-eclampsia, premature delivery and low-birth-weight babies. Not all stresses can be dealt with easily, but do what you can. A large study in Sweden has recently found that the kinds of stress most likely to affect a baby's growth are lack of emotional and practical support, social isolation and an unstable home life. Anything which relaxes you, whether it is yoga, swimming or vegging out in front of the TV, should be a regular part of your routine.

- **Don't forget Dad** While the mother's health plays a major role in the health of her child, fathers are influential as well. Men who smoke are more likely to father children of low birth weight. Those who work in jobs which bring them into contact with pesticides and toxic chemicals are more likely to father children with birth defects. Such men often bring residues from their work home with them, raising their partner's exposure to toxins.

Some 20 different toxic chemicals with the potential to affect sperm quality and production have been found in random samples of men. Contrast this with US evidence suggesting that men who eat organic foods have sperm counts that are twice as high as those who don't.

Chapter 2

Life in the Womb

Pregnancy is a time of transition. It changes your relationship with yourself, with your partner, your family, your friends and with the world. It is a time when women and men embark on a steep learning curve and begin questioning all sorts of things that they took for granted before.

Today, without even thinking, we ingest dozens of harmful chemicals when we eat conventionally grown produce; fertilisers, herbicides, pesticides and fungicides all combine to make so-called 'fresh' food a significant source of poisons. When we eat conventionally reared meats we are ingesting growth hormones and the myriad just-in-case medications given to conventionally farmed animals, in addition to the pesticides, herbicides, fertilisers and fungicides contained in their feed.

Brightly coloured plastics, soft furnishings, vinyl wallpapers, insulation, varnishes, new carpets, upholstery and new mattresses may look modern and clean, but they continually give off toxic formaldehyde gas which is implicated in respiratory problems and has also been shown to be carcinogenic.

Ever had a good whiff of a new book or newspaper? If so, you were inhaling toxic gases from the paper processing and the ink. Thirsty? Tap water has become a significant source of many different toxins including pesticides, hormones, hazardous waste and heavy metals, as well as water-borne parasites. If you live in an area where the water is fluoridated, your water contains a chemical which is more toxic than arsenic and only slightly less toxic than lead.

Many of the things we associate with making our world and ourselves more 'civilised' are the things which cause the most damage. For instance, air fresheners, fertilisers, household disinfectants, hair dyes, even fluoride toothpaste all contribute to a growing toxic load on our bodies. Increasingly, research is showing that exposure to environmental toxins while in the womb may be responsible for a growing number of health problems in childhood as well as later in life.

Many parents-to-be believe that as long as the baby is inside its mother it is safe from environmental toxins. This belief stems from a long-standing view that the placenta – the baby's life support system – acts like a filter, only letting the nutrients and immune protective substance like antibodies into the baby's system. In reality, the placenta is more like a sponge.

It consists of a complex mass of blood vessels (enough to completely cover more than half a tennis court!) which carry nutrients and oxygen to the baby and remove waste products and carbon dioxide. While the placenta can protect your baby to some degree it is not a total barrier, and studies show that today more than 350 man-made toxic chemicals are being passed on to babies in increasing amounts through pathways such as the placenta.

Absolutely *everything* that enters the mother's system enters the baby's system via the placenta. So along with all those vitamins, minerals, amino acids and antibodies comes heavy metals, car fumes, pesticides, cigarette smoke, drugs and the chemicals from household cleaners and cosmetics.

A developing baby is much more sensitive than adults to changes in the supply of nutrients and the presence of poisons. So much so that even if the mother feels well, her child may be struggling to get what it needs to develop.

The WWF in the UK reported that: 'It is now recognised that the foetus can be damaged by relatively low levels of contaminants which do not affect the adult... Exposure in the womb can cause birth defects and can affect our children's future ability to reproduce and their susceptibility to diseases such as cancer. Functional deficits may also be caused, such that some children may not reach their full potential. Put simply, the integrity of the next generation is at stake.'

There is a huge body of evidence to show that a combination of inadequate nutrition and exposure to environmental toxins can have a profound effect on the developing child. For instance:

- According to the National Network to Prevent Birth Defects in the US, a 50 per cent reduction in birth defects could be achieved if parents simply improved their diets and limited their exposure to toxic substances.
- The UK preconceptual care association Foresight has published figures which show that a pre-pregnancy health programme which includes dietary correction and reduction of toxins leads to an overall birth defect rate of less than 1 per cent – compared to 5–7 per cent which is the national average.
- Everyday toxins such as food additives and those in unfiltered, polluted tap waters raise the risk of your baby having a birth defect. Pesticide exposure during pregnancy has been linked to an increase in birth defects and a greater risk of contracting cancer later in life.
- One class of chemicals causing concern at the time of writing is hormone disrupters. These oestrogen-like chemicals are found in large amounts in pesticide residues, as well as in everyday household detergents and toiletries and even in disposable nappies. Scientists are concerned that exposure to these chemicals may alter our children's thyroid function and sexual characteristics. They have already been implicated in low sperm counts in young men and there is a fear that exposure to too many of these synthetic oestrogens may predispose young girls to oestrogen-dependent cancers of the breast, ovary and endometrium (lining of the womb) later in life.

Throughout this book there are practical suggestions for limiting your exposure to environmental toxins in all areas of your life. What becomes obvious is that there is almost no place in our modern world where we don't encounter a potential 'hazard' of some kind. They key is not to panic or become obsessive, but to make healthy changes when and where you can. While nobody can avoid all pollution, it makes sense to try and reduce the total toxic load on your body whenever possible.

Simply being aware of some of the sources of indoor and outdoor pollution can provide you with the wherewithal to make subtle changes in the way you live and work, should you wish to.

Learning to avoid environmental toxins can encompass lots of everyday activities such as not going out on particularly polluted days, installing a water filter, buying organic food or finding alternatives to the full range of chemicals which we use in our homes such as cleaning agents, insecticides, fertilisers, disinfectants and cosmetics. It can mean reducing the number of brightly coloured plastics in the house and thus reducing your exposure to harmful formaldehyde gases and avoiding the use of aerosols – for any purpose – since they make it much easier to inhale harmful chemicals.

What are you eating?

If you want to start cleaning up your environment, begin with what you eat. The food we eat is inexorably linked with our wellbeing. It is the bedrock on which a healthy life is based. It is the body's ready store of nutrients and energy – the thing that holds us up, bolsters our immunity, fights free-radical damage and maintains our energy cycles in the face of an increasingly polluted and stressful world.

We have to eat and drink to live, yet increasingly eating and drinking has become an act of faith because most of what we consume today does not resemble 'food' in any traditional sense of the word.

Indeed, much of what we call food today would only have existed in the realms of science fiction one 100 years ago; exotic items grown without soil, flown in daily from far away, made from ingredients synthesised in a laboratory and preserved long beyond their natural shelf life with a variety of industrial chemicals derived from petroleum by-products.

We eat meat by-products enhanced with artificial meat flavours to make them palatable. We eat processed, quick-cook microwave and oven meals. Even the so-called healthy cereals we eat for breakfast are so highly processed and nutritionally poor that the manufacturers have to add vitamins to them simply so that they can be classified as foods.

These foods also contain myriad additives – occasionally at higher levels than any actual nutrients in them – and contaminants such as pesticides. Today it is estimated that every one of us ingests a gallon of pesticides and herbicides a year from our daily diet.

There are thousands of food additives approved for use in our foods. If your diet is high in processed or convenience foods you will be consuming a staggering amount of these additives and artificial ingredients each year. Sugar, high fructose corn sweeteners (usually found in fizzy drinks), salt, citric acid, pepper, vegetable colours, mustard, yeast and baking soda account for the vast majority – some 98 per cent – of the total amount of food additives we consume. But even though the rest are used in very small amounts, it has been estimated that the average American, for example, consumes about 2.4 kg (5lb) of additives per year. If you include refined sugar – the food processing industry's most used and abused additive – the total skyrockets to 65kg (135lb) a year.

Additives are placed in food for a number of reasons, to facilitate the preparation of processed foods or to lengthen shelf life, for instance. They are also used to make food more appealing. With the use of chemical additives, food technicians are able to mimic natural flavours, colour foods that are well past their nutritional best to make them look more 'natural' or 'fresh', preserve foods for increasingly longer periods of time and create highly manipulated forms of bread, biscuits, fruits, vegetables, meats and dairy products.

Chemicals can also be used to make the product more marketable in some way – for example by adding a sugar substitute a manufacturer can advertise its product as 'sugar free'. Today some 'foods' such as coffee creamers, chewing gums and sweets consist almost entirely of artificial ingredients derived from synthetic chemicals.

Are all additives harmful?

Although we eat them every day, food additives are not subject to the same scrutiny by the regulatory authorities as drugs, and the history of food additives includes a number of products that were once deemed safe but later were banned or allowed to be used only if accompanied by warnings. Certain food colourings, the artificial sweeteners cyclamate and saccharin and the flavour enhancer monosodium glutamate (MSG) are examples of such products.

At their best, additives add little or no nutritional value to a food product. At their worst, they can detract from your health and your day-to-day wellbeing. In addition, some food additives can provoke powerful adverse effects in some people, while appearing to cause no problems for others. For instance, sulphites, a group of preservatives/antioxidants used in dried fruits and wines, are known to cause sensitive individuals (for instance those suffering from asthma) to experience severe reactions.

People with the genetic disorder phenylketonuria (PKU) are unable to fully metabolise the artificial sweetener aspartame; this can lead to a build-up of its breakdown products in their body that can potentially cause serious brain damage. The flavour enhancer MSG, a relative of aspartame and also a neurotoxin, can cause sensitive individuals to experience headache, nausea, weakness and difficulty breathing.

While food additives and preservatives undergo a required series of pre-marketing tests, often with laboratory animals being given huge doses of individual additives, nobody can ever test for what really happens when all the different additives in a food break down and interact with each other in your body.

Avoiding additives

With more than 10,000 chemicals added to our food, it can be a daunting task to decipher labels and decide which products you should and should not be buying. The best way to avoid synthetic chemicals in your food is to buy fresh ingredients and make it yourself. But on those occasions when you do resort to second best, consider avoiding foods that use the following ingredients. In Europe these additives will usually be listed by their 'E number'. In Australia they generally have the same numbers without the E prefix – a system that is due to be adopted internationally in the next few years.

To find them you have to get into the habit of reading food labels as you shop. Don't be fooled into thinking that a high price tag guarantees quality. Some very high-priced brand name convenience foods are full of the worst kinds of additives, while some of the more moderately priced non-brand-name products contain smaller amounts. Equally, some organic foods, especially cakes and biscuits, can contain more sugar and fat than conventional brands.

When shopping for food, try to avoid those products that contain the following additives:

Allura Red AC
E129
- **Found in:** Food colouring in snacks, sauces, preserves, soups, wine, cider

Amaranth
E123
- **Found in:** Food colouring in wine, spirits, fish roe

Aspartame
E951
- **Found in:** Sweetener in snacks, sweets, alcohol, desserts, 'diet foods'

Benzoic acid
E210
- **Found in:** Preservative in many foods, including drinks, low-sugar products, cereals, meat products

Brilliant Black BN
E151
- **Found in:** Food colouring in drinks, sauces, snacks, wines, cheese

Butylated Hydroxy-anisole
E320
- **Found in:** Preservative, particularly in fat-containing foods, confectionery, meats

Calcium benzoate
E213
- **Found in:** Preservative in many foods, including drinks, low-sugar products, cereals, meat products

Calcium sulphite
E226
- **Found in:** Preservative in a vast array of foods from burgers to biscuits, frozen mushrooms to horseradish. Used to make old produce look fresh

Carboxymethyl cellulose sodium salt
E466
- **Found in:** Bulking agent found in ice creams, beverages and other foods

Carrageenan (seaweed extract)
E407
- **Found in:** Thickener used in wide variety of foods including dressings, ice cream, cheese spreads, jams and custard

Monosodium glutamate (MSG)
E621
- **Found in:** Flavour enhancer found in almost every processed food

Nitrite chemicals
E249–252
- **Found in:** Curing agents commonly found in cured or preserved meats

Polyoxyethylene sorbitan chemicals
E432–436
- **Found in:** Emulsifiers found in spreads, cake mixes, dressings, deserts and beverages

Ponceau 4R, Cochineal Red A
E124
- **Found in:** Food colouring found in sweets, desserts and beverages

Potassium benzoate
E212
- **Found in:** See calcium benzoate

Potassium nitrate
E249
- **Found in:** Preservative in cured meats and canned meat products

Propyl p-hydroxybenzoate, propylparaben, parabens
E216
- **Found in:** Preservative in cereals, snacks, pâté, meat products, confectionery

Saccharin and its sodium, potassium and calcium salts
E954
- **Found in:** Sweetener in diet and no-sugar products

Sodium metabisulphite
E223
- **Found in:** Preservative and antioxidant used in dried and frozen fruits and fruit fillings

Sodium sulphite
E221
- **Found in:** Preservative used in winemaking and other processed foods

Soya protein isolates
None
- **Found in:** Protein source widely used in ready meals and bread

Stannous chloride (tin)
E512
- **Found in:** Antioxidant and colour-retention agent in canned and bottled foods, fruit juices

Sulphur dioxide
E220
- **Found in:** Preservative found in dried fruits and condiments

Sunset Yellow FCF, Orange Yellow S
E110
- **Found in:** Food colouring found in sweets, desserts and beverages

Tartrazine
E102
- **Found in:** Yellow food colouring found in sweets, desserts and beverages

Tri- and Polyphosphate chemicals
E450(b)
- **Found in:** Added to meat to make it take up water to increase the weight (and thus the price)

Hidden additives
Apart from the known additives that are listed on the label, modern processed foods also contain a number of unintentional contaminants such as pesticides and genetically modified (GM) ingredients. These 'hidden additives' can have a profound effect on health. Since they are generally industrial chemicals, food will not be your only source of exposure to them. That's why choosing to cut your exposure to them whenever and wherever you can makes sense.

Health professionals recommend that you eat at least five servings of fruit and vegetables every day as part of a varied diet. Unfortunately, if you eat conventionally grown produce, you may also be unknowingly ingesting a mixture of harmful pesticides including:

- insecticides to control insects
- rodenticides to control rodents
- herbicides to control weeds
- fungicides to control mould and fungus
- antimicrobials to control bacteria

Just because you can't see or taste them doesn't mean they aren't there. The most comprehensive testing for the presence of unwanted chemicals in food is the ongoing US Total Diet Study (TDS), conducted by the US Food and Drug Administration (FDA) and updated yearly. The TDS looks for the presence of many different chemicals in food, but its findings on levels of chlorinated pesticides have been particularly distressing. In its 1988 report, DDE (a close relative of DDT) was found in every single sample of raisins, spinach (fresh and frozen), chilli con carne and beef.

DDE was also found in 93 per cent of processed cheese, mince, hot dogs, collards (spring greens), chicken, turkey and ice-cream sandwiches sampled. It was also present in 87 per cent of lamb chops, salami, canned spinach, meatloaf and butter, and in 81 per cent of sauces and creamed spinach.

Growing crops or rearing animals on land contaminated with banned substances means we 'recycle' these toxins back into the food chain

Given that DDT and DDE have been banned in the US since 1972, it is likely that some of this contamination is from produce imported from other countries that still use these chemicals. But some of it is also because of the persistence of these chemicals in our soil: growing crops or rearing animals on land contaminated with DDT and DDE means that we 'recycle' these toxins back into the food chain.

In the intervening years, things didn't get much better. The 1999 TDS showed that, among the foods sampled, 17 different pesticides were found in butter, 32 different ones in cherries, 29 in strawberries and 27 in apples. The baked potato samples contained 23 pesticides and the hamburger sample 22. Milk chocolate samples contained 18 different pesticides. Once again, DDE/DDT was the residue most often found, with chlorpyrifos-methyl, malathion, endosulfan, dieldrin and chlorpyrifos also being very common.

In the UK, the 1999 Annual Report by the Working Party on Pesticide Residues (WPPR) found that 27 per cent of the full range of foods tested showed pesticide residues. Among them, DDT (which is banned in the UK) was found in beef slices, corned beef and lamb's kidney, and 2,4-D (also banned in the UK) was found in over half the oranges tested. Oranges, pears, lettuces, chocolate and apples contained the highest numbers and levels of residues. Three-quarters of the chocolate samples contained lindane (a relative of DDT), and one in eight jars of baby food was also contaminated. Surveys in Australia and New Zealand have found similarly high levels of pesticides in foods.

Pesticides are harmful to people – no one could reasonably dispute that. We can't always detect the immediate health effects from eating pesticide-laden food, but that doesn't mean that they are safe. The World Health Organization (WHO) estimates that between 3.5 and 5 million people globally suffer acute pesticide poisoning every year. Studies of people regularly exposed to pesticides show that they can cause nerve damage, cancer, diabetes and other effects that can take a long time to develop.

All these effects depend on how toxic the pesticide is and how much of it is consumed. When researchers test the amount of pesticide in a single carrot or apple and declare that it is too low to be harmful – they are also missing the point. In the real world we do not eat foods singly. We eat them in quantity and in combination day in and day out.

What can you do?

Once they are on or in food, pesticides are very difficult to avoid. Some authorities recommend that we wash and scrub all fresh fruits and vegetables thoroughly under running water. Running water has an abrasive effect that soaking does not have, which may help remove traces of chemicals from the surface of fruits vegetables and dirt from crevices. Not all pesticide residues can be removed by washing because many are designed to be water-resistant so they won't wash off crops when it rains.

Peeling the skin off fruits and vegetables whenever possible and discarding the outer leaves of leafy vegetables can reduce your exposure. Trimming the fat from meat, and the skin from poultry and fish will also help as most pesticide residues collect in fat.

Eating a variety of food is also sometimes recommended to help reduce your exposure to any single pesticide. It is uncertain how effective this is since most pesticides function in similar ways and since on the journey from farm to table many foods are coated with multiple pesticides and fungicides. From a health standpoint however, eating food from a variety of sources will give you a more comprehensive mix of nutrients and this may have a protective effect.

In fact the best, and probably the only, way to avoid pesticides in your food is to include as much organic, non-genetically modified food in your diet as is possible.

GM ingredients

Increasingly, headlines about genetic modification leave many of us anxious and confused about the food we eat. We now have the technology to alter the most basic building blocks of life. Unfortunately, we have not conducted the studies necessary to prove or disprove the safety of GM foods over either the long or the short term.

Some crops of rapeseed now contain human genes

We are unaware of whether GM foods can for instance cause damage to a vulnerable human foetus at certain stages of development – though animal tests show this is entirely possible. GM foods don't taste better and they are not cheaper to buy; they have, however, been implicated in increased resistance to antibiotics and the growth of super bugs. They have also been linked to an increased incidence of allergies.

Food can either be genetically modified itself, or contain genetically modified ingredients. The issues are very complex, but if you are concerned, you might consider avoiding or limiting:

- **Tomatoes (and tomato purée)** were the first GM foods to be sold. In the US you can buy fresh tomatoes which have been genetically modified, in the UK you can only buy purée made from these tomatoes. Watch out for ready-made foods such as pizza which may use GM tomato purée.
- **Soya** has been modified to resist weed killer. In the US, suppliers of most of the world's soya, GM soya and unmodified soya are not kept separately, and processed foods may contain both. Soya is present in most baked and pre-packaged foods in several forms: oil (often just labelled vegetable oil), vegetable fat, flour, lecithin and vegetable protein.
- **Maize** has been modified so that it contains a bacteria toxic to a common crop pest. Maize is used as a grain, as corn (or maize) flour, corn meal, corn starch, corn syrup, dextrose, glucose, fructose, xanthan gum, maltodextrin and as corn oil. Be aware of things like chocolate bars and sweet drinks which contain sugars derived from maize.
- **Cheese** can be made with a GM enzyme called chymosin instead of traditional rennet. Chymosin is used in many vegetarian cheeses and increasingly in hard cheeses for general consumption.

A RETURN TO REAL FOOD

During pregnancy your diet is of real importance. Getting into the good food habit now makes it easier to teach our children by example as they grow.

The more we learn about the toxic potential of modern foods, the greater the need for a new food culture that values wholesomeness, nutrition, freshness and flavour. Raising our expectations of food and embracing these values has the knock-on effect of protecting the natural environment, treating animals humanely, protecting our soil, and respecting the farmers and food industry workers who are involved in the food-production process. It also leads to a stronger preference for foods that are produced locally.

Getting back to good food is much easier than you think. Consider these tips:

- **Eat the best quality you can afford.** Avoid junk food (such as biscuits, confectionery and fizzy drinks), which are not only chock-full of artificial colours and other additives, but are also of little nutritional value – high in calories, sugar, fats and/or sodium. This is especially good advice for children, who are the main consumers of junk foods and are at increased risk if there are any health problems with additives. In addition, while freezing foods can be convenient, freezing also destroys vital nutrients (research shows that up to a quarter of vitamin C and one half of folate in fruits and vegetables can be lost in the freezing and that levels of other important antioxidants can decline by 20–30 per cent); there is even some indication that refrigeration has a similar effects.
- **Eat freshly prepared.** Consider removing the microwave from your kitchen. If you only use it to heat coffee, or cook potatoes or pre-packaged meals, you probably don't need it. Getting rid of your microwave will also vastly improve the quality of the food you eat since food that has been microwaved has fewer nutrients in it. In addition, proteins, such as those found as meats, are significantly altered during the microwave process. Eating food directly from the microwave may also mean ingesting food that is still giving off radiation; this is why users are advised to let food 'sit' for a few minutes afterwards – to let all this radiation disperse.

Ctd

- **Eat natural.** If it comes in a box, a tub, tray or a jar – or if it is a colour you don't normally see in nature, think twice before putting it in your mouth.
- **Eat variety.** This may limit your exposure to any one additive – safer in the event that it turns out to have long-term health risks.
- **Eat seasonally.** It is less expensive, provides greater variety in the diet and will reduce your exposure to antifungal and anti-bacterial chemicals commonly used to extend the shelf life of products grown out of season or shipped halfway across the globe.
- **Eat slowly.** If it's a choice between a burger bar or the local cafe or restaurant, ditch the burger bar. If it's a choice between wolfing down a sandwich at your desk or sitting on a park bench, go to the park. Wherever possible try to sit down and enjoy your meal, and teach your children how to do the same.
- **Eat what you like.** Be guided by your tastes and be aware that the more you change your eating habits the more your tastes will start to return to normal. Cravings for salty, sugary, highly processed foods will disappear and with them the tendency to overeat foods that are not good for your health.

- **Enzymes** are used in a large number of products including drinks, bakery goods and dairy products. Manufacturers are not obliged to include these on the product information.
- **Canola, or rapeseed**, is mainly used as an oil. Some crops now contain human genes.
- **Yeast** which has been genetically modified has been approved for making bread, but it is difficult to know the extent to which it is used in bakery products.
- **Vitamin B2**, known as riboflavin, is now widely produced from genetically modified micro-organisms. It is generally added to breakfast cereals, soft drinks, baby foods and diet foods.
- **E numbers** indicate preservatives, flavourings and colourings. Watch out for E101, E101a, E150, E153, E161c, E322, E471, E621 all of which may be GM derivatives.

To spot GM foods you will have to become a reader of labels. Even this will not guarantee that your diet will be GM-free. Labelling laws in the UK and in the US are very confused and seem to exist mostly to protect the manufacturer rather than the consumer. There is no requirement to label a product which may contain GM ingredients, flavouring or additives, and only a very few volunteer this information. For the moment, the best way to avoid GM foods is to eat as much organic and freshly prepared (by you, in your home) food as possible.

Cleaning without chemicals

Most of us tend to think of our homes as havens, and environmental pollution as a problem that is 'out there'. Perhaps there was a time

CAN CLEANING PRODUCTS CAUSE ASTHMA?

Household chemicals, including bleach, disinfectant and cleaning fluid, have been blamed for the huge surge in childhood asthma and data suggests that the chemical formaldehyde present in many household cleaners could be the reason. A December 2004 British study of more than 7,000 children found that children born into households which use them most are twice as likely to suffer persistent wheezing, which is often a precursor to asthma.

The findings echoed those of a 2004 Australian study that also linked volatile chemicals in household chemicals with asthma. According to these studies, the following household products were the ones most likely to trigger an asthma attack:

- Disinfectant
- Bleach
- Aerosols
- Air freshener
- Window cleaner
- Carpet cleaner

- Paint or varnish
- White spirit
- Pesticide
- Paint stripper
- Dry-cleaning fluid

when this was true. But not any more. Today some of the most toxic chemicals we come into contact with are not blown in through the window from some anonymous factory or a passing car. They are bought in good faith in stores and supermarkets and brought back into our homes by us.

Indoor air pollution is a problem on the rise and since most of us spend 90 per cent of our time indoors – in homes, offices and schools – it's a problem that can contribute substantially to poor health. The air indoors can be contaminated by any number of things, from the presence of a smoker to the use of formaldehyde-laden particleboard furnishings. But a primary cause, according to the US Environmental Protection Agency, is the use of conventional household cleaners.

In order to fulfil the increasingly ambitious claims for their products, manufacturers rely on combinations of chemicals that can be harsh and highly toxic. Many of these easily evaporate or give off gases that can contaminate indoor air. Ask yourself, if a cleaner can instantly strip a kitchen tile of years of accumulated grease, what might it do to your skin or to your body's cells, or to the natural environment if you happen to breathe it in?

Because of their association with good hygiene, household cleaning agents are the most deceptive of indoor pollutants. While many people are aware that these products can contain allergens, few are aware that they can contain other substances that have the potential to affect human health in other, more substantial, ways.

But everyday cleaning products can, for instance, contain carcinogens, hormone-disrupting chemicals, central nervous system disrupters, reproductive toxins and psychoactive chemicals (substances that alter brain function). The awful truth, in many cases, is that when we wash our clothes, dishes and floors with them, we are using hazardous waste to wash away simple dirt.

Because household cleaners aren't required to carry full ingredient labels you will have to look for 'signal words' on the label that help you know what kind of cleaner you are using. You know it's toxic if the label carries words like 'Hazardous', 'Corrosive', 'Inflammable', 'Warning', 'Caution', 'Danger' and 'Irritant'. Products like these will contain one or more of the following ingredients:

Alcohol (including ethanol, methanol, isopropanol)
- **Effect:** Nausea and vomiting if swallowed.

Ammonia
- **Effect:** Fatal when swallowed

Ammonium Hydroxide
- **Effect:** Corrosive, irritant

Butyl cellosolve
- **Effect:** Damages liver, kidney and central nervous system (CNS) damage

Chlorine
- **Effect:** Eye, skin and lung irritant. Major cause of poisonings in children

Formaldehyde
- **Effect:** Highly toxic; known carcinogen

Hydrochloric acid
- **Effect:** Corrosive, eye and skin irritant

Lye
- **Effect:** Severe damage to stomach and oesophagus if swallowed

Naptha
- **Effect:** Depresses the central nervous system

Nitrobenzene
- **Effect:** Causes skin discoloration, shallow breathing, vomiting and death

Paradichlorobenzenes
- **Effect:** Irritates eyes, nose, central nervous system

Petroleum distillates
- **Effect:** Highly inflammable; suspected carcinogen

Phenol
- **Effect:** Extremely dangerous; suspected carcinogen and fatal if taken internally

Propellants
- **Effect:** Central nervous system poisons, irregular heartbeat.

Propylene glycol
- **Effect:** Irritant and immunotoxin

Sodium tripolyphosphate
- **Effect:** Skin, eye and lung irritant

Trichloroethane
- **Effect:** Damages liver and kidneys; narcotic

Greener cleaning

Not many of us love to do housework. It can be time consuming, it can be messy and it can be back breaking. But it is also a necessary part of keeping our homes hygienic and habitable. A clean home is a healthy home. But while many of us scrub and dust and polish to keep dirt and germs at bay, the truth is that many of the products we use to achieve a clean and germ-free home are more risky than the germs and the dirt themselves.

It is ironic, for instance, that while most modern cleaning products will remove surface dirt and sometimes germs, they make the air and surfaces dirty with industrial chemicals, hydrocarbons, chlorine and more.

While most of us sympathise with the need to keep environmental pollution to an absolute minimum, our resolve can disappear at the supermarket where brightly packaged products promise to transform our homes into spotlessly clean aromatherapy spas. What could green cleaning possibly have to offer that could compete with today's modern formulations? Well for starters:

- **It costs less** – by using readily available ingredients like baking soda and vinegar to clean your home you will find you spend less on everyday cleaners.
- **Less backache** – when you make it yourself there are no heavy bottles to carry home. Suddenly bringing in the groceries becomes less taxing.
- **No heavy perfumes** – fragrances used in cleaning products are significant triggers of asthma as well as headaches. Going fragrance-free may have the knock-on effect of improving your health.
- **Self-sufficiency** – not having to rely on commercial cleaners is very liberating. Suddenly you will view all those commercials that try to sell you toilet cleaner as a cure for a dead-end love-life in a new light.
- **A genuinely cleaner home** – instead of washing away dirt with synthetic chemicals, or masking unpleasant smells with other smells, you will really be getting your home clean.
- **Nothing dangerous under the sink** – a much safer way to live, especially if you have children.
- **A cleaner planet** – you'll be doing your bit, relatively effortlessly, to keep the planet in good shape for future generations.

Most of us are in the habit of buying cleaning products in the supermarket – so when we start to look for alternatives the first place we turn is back to the supermarket shelves, where genuinely green alternatives are often pretty scarce.

Why not break a bad habit and try making your own? The simplest ingredients from your kitchen are often all that is needed for the majority of household cleaning jobs.

- **Baking soda** – a versatile product that is safe enough to drink (it's a common heartburn remedy) and brush your teeth with (it has a gentle whitening action). Used dry, or mixed with water and a tiny squirt of washing-up liquid, it is a disinfectant and mild abrasive that can remove hardened dirt and grease without scratching surfaces. It also softens water, helping your other cleaners, including laundry detergents, clean and rinse more effectively.
- **Vinegar** – also known as acetic acid, vinegar is a mild acid that

cuts grease, disinfects and discourages mould. It is also an efficient air freshener.

- **Soap** – real soap is made from natural products like vegetable oils and animal fats. It is an effective cleaning agent that biodegrades quickly and has a minimal impact on the environment. Second best is an environmentally friendly washing-up liquid.

- **Borax** – an effective water softener and can be used in home-made products to help soap work harder and rinse better. It is a useful mould and mildew remover and disinfectant and can be used to help whiten clothes. While it is a very effective cleaner it should be used with caution around children because, unlike baking soda, it is toxic if swallowed.

- **Microfibre cleaning cloths** – the basic purpose of detergents is to bring more water – one of the most efficient solvents in the world – into contact with whatever surface you are cleaning. Microfibres, which are finer than human hair and have amazing absorbency, effectively do the same thing. Used as directed they will leave most surfaces both clean and dry and leave you wondering why you ever used any other type of cloth. When buying a microfibre cloth remember that the most effective ones have densely packed fibres. They are more costly than run-of-the-mill cleaning cloths, but are good value in the long run since they can be reused indefinitely.

- **Elbow grease** – many kitchen cupboard cleaning ingredients work just as well as the harsh chemicals in ready-made products. But occasionally using non-toxic alternatives will mean you have let go of the idea of 'wash and go' and 'spray and wipe' and apply a little more muscle, or a little more patience, to get the job done.

Toxic toiletries

Certain everyday toiletries may also pose a threat to your unborn child's health. There is a substantial body of evidence to show that hairdressers are at greater risk of having babies with malformations than other women, and that they are more prone to miscarriage as well. This is because hair dressers are exposed daily to the poisonous chemicals in hair preparations such as shampoo, conditioners, hair sprays, gels, mousses and hair dyes.

The average woman is not exposed to these chemicals in the same concentration, but a quick look at your bathroom cupboard might give pause for thought. If it is filled with lots of different types of hair-care products, you might consider cutting down.

Similarly, a UK study of 14,000 women revealed that pregnant women who constantly use aerosol products such as air fresheners, deodorants, furniture polishes and hair sprays have significantly higher rates of headaches and post-natal depression than who use these products less than once a week. The high-users' babies had higher rates of ear infections and diarrhoea.

Our everyday toiletries and cosmetics are comprised of literally hundreds of chemicals. It is estimated that the average woman is exposed to 200 unique man-made chemicals every day, just through her toiletries and cosmetics. Not all of them are bad for you but some are. You can absorb up to 60 per cent of whatever you put onto your skin, so cutting down on unnecessary toiletries is a healthy habit to get into. Getting to grips with the potentially harmful ingredients in your own toiletries may also help you resist the temptation to smother your baby with the unnecessary and harsh chemicals contained in many baby products (see Chapter 4).

It can be hard to know what to avoid, especially if you have only just started reading the labels of the products you buy. So here's a 'baker's (dirty) dozen' of ingredients that can be found in everyday products for men, women and children, which you should try to avoid if you can.

Aluminium
- **Look for:** Aluminium chlorohydrate, Aluminium zirconium
- **Which products:** Deodorants and make-up products
- **Toxic effects:** Neurotoxin linked to Alzheimer's disease. May also contribute to heart and lung disease and fertility problems.

Antibacterials
- **Look for:** Triclosan, Benzalknium chloride, Chlorohexidine
- **Which products:** Antibacterial hand cleaners
- **Toxic effects:** Skin irritation, promotes bacterial resistance

Colours and dyes
- **Look for:** Ingredients starting 'CT' followed by numbers
- **Which products:** Any coloured product, including make-up
- **Toxic effects:** Skin irritation and allergies. Many synthetic dyes can cause cancer in animals.

Detergent
- **Look for:** Ammonium lauryl sulphate, Cocamide DEA, Cocamide MEA, Sodium lauryl sulphate, Cocamidopropyl betaine
- **Which products:** Shampoo, body wash, bubble bath, liquid hand soap.
- **Toxic effects:** Skin irritation, can promote formation of carcinogenic nitrosamines in products during storage (see PEG below)

Fragrances
- **Look for:** Parfum
- **Which products:** Nearly all cosmetics
- **Toxic effects:** Parfum is a mixture of dozens of synthetic fragrances. Linked with asthma, skin irritation, nausea, mood changes, depression, lethargy, irritability and memory lapses.

Mineral oil
- **Look for:** Paraffinum liquidum, Petrolatum
- **Which products:** Face and body lotions, baby oils
- **Toxic effects:** Skin irritation, allergen, potential carcinogen

Phthalates
- **Look for:** Dibutyl phthalate (DBP)
- **Which products:** Hair spray and nail varnish, as well as fragranced products
- **Toxic effects:** Hormone-disrupting plasticisers that 'fix' the fragrance onto the skin. Can cause damage to liver, lungs and kidneys. May affect fertility and foetal development.

Preservatives
- **Look for:** Parabens, EDTA, Formaldehyde, Quaternium 15
- **Which products:** All conventional cosmetics and toiletries
- **Toxic effects:** Associated with skin irritation and allergic reactions. Can be neurotoxic. Some, like parabens, are suspected hormone disruptors.

Polyethylene glycol
- **Look for:** PEG
- **Which products:** Moisturisers, body lotions, shampoos, conditioners, deodorants, make-up
- **Toxic effects:** Skin irritation, can be contaminated with the carcinogen 1,4-dioxane. PEGs can also form carcinogenic nitrosamines when mixed with detergents like DEA and TEA.

Propylene glycol
- **Look for:** PPG
- **Which products:** Soaps, cleansers
- **Toxic effects:** Skin irritation, aggravates eczema, potential neurotoxin

Silicones
- **Look for:** Cyclomethicone, Cyclopentasiloxnem Dimethicone, Simethicone
- **Which products:** Body lotions and creams, hair conditioner, most make-up
- **Toxic effects:** Prolonged exposure causes irritation. Some emollients are known tumour promoters and accumulate in liver and lymph nodes. Non-biodegradable.

Sunscreens
- **Look for:** benzophenone-3, homosalate 4-methyl-benzylidene camphor (4-MBC), octyl-methoxycinnamate, octyl-dimethyl-PABA, octocrylene.
- **Which products:** Suncare products, face and body moisturisers, lipsticks, foundations
- **Toxic effects:** Hormone-disrupting chemicals, known to affect fertility of animals in the wild.

Talc

- **Look for:** Talc
- **Which products:** Body powder, face powder, eye shadow, blusher
- **Toxic effects:** Respiratory irritant. In body powder it is linked to ovarian cancer.

LOOKING GOOD – ORGANIC MATERNITY CLOTHES

When you are pregnant, the extra weight you are carrying and the fact that your blood volume doubles means that you can feel boiling hot even in the dead of winter. This is a good time to discover the pleasures of clothes made from natural fabrics. Unlike synthetics, clothes made from cotton, linen, silk and wool allow the body to breathe, keeping it cool on warm days and warm on cool days.

Many companies now produce clothes made from organic fibres. There are some good reasons why mums-to-be might consider making the switch. Most modern clothing is treated with chemicals to help it keep its appearance and to act as a flame retardant (see Chapter 5).

These invisible chemicals, which include pesticide residues, dyes and fabric treatments, can be highly toxic. For example, the flame retardant used in modern clothing is a known carcinogen that can be absorbed into the system via the skin. Once this happens it is also absorbed into your baby's system.

At the end of this book is a list of several companies who supply organic clothing suitable for mums-to-be. By including just a few non-toxic items in your wardrobe you will be making significant inroads into cutting down the total toxic load on your body.

Adding clothes made from organic
fibres to your wardrobe will help cut down
your toxic load

Chemicals at work

Even if you don't work in a job which directly brings you into contact with noxious and toxic chemicals, you may be exposed to more poisons than you realise at your work place.

Over 25,000 individual chemicals are used in industry with a further 2,000 compounds being added each year. If you are worried about exposure to chemicals in the workplace, consulting your GP may not be very helpful. This is a specialist area which may be best discussed with your company's health and safety office or union official. There are special codes of practice which apply to pregnant women and if you think you are working with toxic chemicals you are entitled to arrange alternative work with your employer with no loss of pay or benefits. Since toxic chemicals can enter the mother's body after pregnancy and birth and be passed on in breastmilk, these arrangements should continue for as long as you are breastfeeding.

The chemicals which most women encounter at work include:

- Metals – for example lead, mercury and copper
- Gases – such as carbon monoxide but also the off-gassing of formaldehyde from carpets, furniture and plastics

KEEP IT OUTDOORS

Take your shoes off when you're in the house. This will help minimise the risk of bringing pesticides and other harmful chemicals into the house where they linger in the carpet and can be inhaled. Try using any of the organic alternatives to garden pesticides and fungicides that are currently on the market.

- Passive smoking
- Insecticides
- Herbicides
- Solvents – for example carbon tetrachloride but also those used in cleaning fluids and solutions
- Drugs during their manufacture
- Disinfecting agents – such as ethylene oxide
- Fragrances – such as those used in air fresheners and cleaning fluids

A recent study showed that women who work with organic solvents – for instance artists, graphic designers, laboratory technicians, veterinary technicians, cleaners, factory and office workers and chemists – have a greatly increased risk both of miscarriage and of giving birth to premature, low-birth-weight or damaged babies.

Of course, these kinds of solvents are not restricted to the workplace. They are also common in the home in cleaning products, toiletries and paints. Information elsewhere within this book can help you choose alternatives which are safer for you and your child.

Avoiding toxic metals

Among the most potentially harmful substances to a developing baby are toxic metals like lead, cadmium, aluminium and mercury – environmental pollutants which can enter the body through inhalation or through the food we eat. The greater the mother's exposure, the greater the risk to her child because though these pollutants build up slowly in your body over time, they are slow to clear from your system. Some, like mercury, never leave the body.

- **Lead** is found in most water supplies as well as in the emissions from car engines and factories. It can get into your system through breathing in polluted air; it can also be absorbed through the skin. Women should be aware that if their partners work in jobs where they are exposed to high levels of lead (plumbers, painters and motor mechanics, for example) then they can become contaminated with lead through her partner's semen. Once you are pregnant you might consider using a condom to avoid lead being absorbed into your body from your partner's seminal fluid.

Lead can also be present in the food you eat since plants and animals may also have been exposed to these pollutants during their growth. Lead contamination has been associated with deformed and dead sperm, infertility, repeated miscarriage and stillbirth. It may also be linked with low birth weight. High levels of lead in pregnant women can predispose their children to dental caries.

To reduce your intake of lead (if you still have lead pipes in your home), consider having a reverse osmosis water filter installed. If this proves too expensive, make sure you run the tap a minute or two before you use the water from it for cooking or drinking.

A healthy diet will help combat the effects of lead. Make sure your diet is rich in foods with vitamins A, C (including bioflavonoids), D and E, and the minerals iron, calcium, magnesium, manganese, selenium, chromium and zinc, as well as protein and fibre. Eating lots of fresh garlic can also help combat the effects of excessive lead.

- **Cadmium** has been linked with both stillbirth and low birth weight. The most common source is cigarette smoke – yours and other people's. It is also present in drinking water, certain plastics and paints (especially with a red or orange colour), enamelled cookware and some insecticides. In addition, there can be cadmium in refined cereal products such as white flour and bread, alcohol, oysters, gelatine, some canned foods, pigs' kidneys from animals treated with a worm killer containing cadmium, and caffeinated drinks such as cola, tea and coffee.

  To avoid cadmium overload, avoid cigarette smoke, even the passive kind. You might consider changing your enamelled pans as well since cadmium can be released during cooking. Keep your diet low in refined foods and be aware that alcoholic drinks may contain cadmium as a preservative – another good reason to cut down or quit during pregnancy.

- **Aluminium** is toxic in high quantities. It may even cause the deterioration of placental function. Every time you cook in an aluminium saucepan you expose yourself to this toxic metal. If the food you are cooking is acidic (such as apples, spinach or rhubarb) it can cause more metal to be released into the food. Many pressure cookers are made with aluminium and this cooking method can also concentrate the metal in your food. Eat food heated in tin foil or served up in freezer-to-oven foil trays to a minimum.

Aluminium is also used as an anti-caking or bleaching agent in foods you use every day such as salt, milk substitute and flour. It may also be present in high levels in your drinking water. Some antiperspirants contain aluminium and although the manufacturers claim that this is unlikely to be absorbed into your blood stream, this has not been proven. It is also present in antacids.

To minimise your exposure to aluminium, steer clear of cooking utensils made from this metal. Make sure foil coverings are not touching fatty foods during cooking. Avoid bleached white flour products and foods containing the additive 556 (aluminium calcium silicate) E173 (aluminium) and 554 (aluminium sodium silicate). Food rich in manganese will help counteract the harmful effects of aluminium (see Appendix 1).

- **Mercury** interferes with placental function. Mercury affects the central nervous system and children with high levels of mercury may also be prone to health disorders such as allergies. There is mercury in our drinking water and you can also ingest it by eating tinned fish. Weed killers and fungicides also contain mercury. But perhaps the biggest source of mercury is the fillings in your teeth. It is now widely accepted that dental amalgam leaks over time, releasing toxic metal into your body.

One answer is to have your metal fillings replaced by composite ones. This can prove to be expensive, although there is no rule which says you have to do it all at one time! It is best to have fillings removed before conception. Don't attempt to have them removed during pregnancy since airborne particles of the drilled mercury can be inhaled and get back into your system via your lungs. Instead, do what you can to reduce your mercury intake, for instance by avoiding canned foods, especially fish. There is some evidence that eating plenty of garlic will help limit mercury absorption.

How to grow a healthy baby – Part II

Pregnancy can be a consciousness-raising experience in many ways, and many women and their partners first become aware of the impact of everyday toxins, for instance in what we eat and drink and in medicines and other drugs we take, at this time.

While it is easy assume the role of a victim and to think of environmental toxins as something that we consume involuntarily, not all toxins come from 'out there'. Many are the result of things that we allow into our homes and into our bodies without giving them a second thought. If you are pregnant or trying to conceive this is a good time to take stock and think about breaking habits that may be affecting your health and that of your unborn child.

Though you may not be able to do anything about pollution from factories or cars, what you eat, drink and breathe are largely within your control. To limit your developing child's exposure to toxins, consider some of the following simple steps:

- **Start reading labels** – on everything. Use the information in this book to make a list of ingredients that you wish to avoid and take this with you when you go shopping.
- **Eat organic foods**, which are free from pesticide residues, food additives and GM ingredients. Organic foods are also significantly higher in nutrients. One US study found that organic tomatoes had 500 per cent more calcium in them than the conventional variety. You'll also get more iron, potassium, magnesium, manganese and copper in every bite as well, which is good for you and your baby.

  If you're thinking of making the switch to organic but budgeting is an issue, then consider buying organic for those foods you eat the most of. Even a small switch to organic teas and coffee (preferably decaffeinated) can substantially reduce your intake of pesticides. Or you may wish to replace the most contaminated types of conventional foods with organic alternatives. This means dairy products and meats (especially beef and offal). Watch out also for orchard fruits such as strawberries, cherries, apricots and apples. Research into pesticides residues on produce shows that these types of fruits are among the most heavily contaminated.
- **Cut out caffeine**. You probably don't think of caffeine as a toxin, but in large quantities, especially when you are pregnant, it is. Caffeine, which is found in coffee, tea, fizzy drinks and chocolate,

leaches essential nutrients out of your system, leaving little for your baby to grow on.

The most recent medical evidence suggests that consuming large amounts of coffee daily – five to six cups – can encourage miscarriage. What isn't known is whether this risk is higher in some women than in others. Caffeine also dehydrates the body. This means that the relative concentration of toxins in your blood will be higher than in a woman who limits caffeine. Instead of caffeinated beverages try drinking herbal teas, or grain coffees such as dandelion and chicory.

- **Limit or avoid cured meats** such as hot dogs, salami, bacon and smoked fish. These are treated with known carcinogens called nitrites. Prenatal exposure to nitrites raises the risk of your child developing cancer. For example, it has been found that men who regularly consume hot dogs run the risk of fathering children at increased risk of leukaemia. Women who eat cured meats during pregnancy appear to increase their child's risk of developing brain cancer. Read the labels on organic cured meats carefully as organic standards have recently been changed to allow the use of nitrites in cured meats.

- **Avoid alcohol** especially in the crucial preconceptual stage and during the first few months of life in the womb. Binge drinking and chronic alcoholism can deplete your body of nutrients such as vitamin B6, iron and zinc, and interfere with normal hormonal function. It also interferes with the proper formation of organs such as the kidneys and raises the risk of congenital malformations.

    There is also evidence to show that consuming alcohol can interfere with a woman's ability to conceive. Once pregnant it can stop your baby developing properly. There are no official rules for preconceptual and prenatal drinking but government guidelines suggest that pregnant women should not drink more than one or two units of alcohol (1 unit equals one small glass of wine) once or twice a week. Nevertheless, many women still prefer to avoid alcohol while trying to conceive and during the first trimester when the foetus is developing.

- **Rethink soft drinks**. Fizzy drinks like cola, lemonade and squash provide empty calories and have the potential to cause harm. They contain caffeine but also sugar which can significantly depress immune functions and leech nutrients from the body. They can also contain artificial sweeteners such as aspartame and other harmful ingredients such as phosphoric acid.

Artificial sweeteners have been shown to harm the developing brain of young animals and scientists now feel it is likely that it does the same to developing human babies. They have also been shown to increase your sweet tooth so ultimately these calorie-sparing drinks may defeat their purpose.

Recently, US researchers have identified a link between soft-drink consumption and brittle bones in teenagers. They are now turning their attention to what happens when mothers consume large quantities of phosphoric acid during the developmentally sensitive time in the womb. Phosphoric acid blocks the absorption of calcium and magnesium by your intestines, which means less is available for your developing baby's bones. As an alternative try experimenting with herbal teas over ice, or fresh fruit juices diluted with sparkling or still water.

- **Stop smoking**. Smoking poisons your body with carcinogenic nicotine and the toxic metal cadmium. When pregnant it decreases the flow of blood and oxygen to the placenta and reduces the availability of essential amino acids necessary for proper growth. Smokers are also twice as likely as non-smokers to miscarry and have ectopic pregnancies. According to recent data, smokers have a 78 per cent higher risk of giving birth to a baby with cleft palate or lip.

    Babies of smokers are also more likely to have chronic breathing problems. Studies have shown that the lungs of babies whose parents smoke are 10 per cent smaller than those of non-smokers, and that their risk of cancer is 50 per cent greater. Babies of smokers are born with fewer natural reserves to fight off infection and have a 43 per cent higher risk of blood disorders, nervous system and sense disorders, bladder and kidney problems and skin disorders, than children of non-smokers.

- **Make your own cleaning products** from simple, non-toxic ingredients. Avoid the use of pump or aerosol sprays, which can make inhaling toxic chemicals much easier.

- **Go natural**. Your skin is likely to be in great condition while you are pregnant – show it off. Limit make-up and when buying toiletries be choosy. Look for those that are certified organic or which contain all-natural ingredients.
- **If you work with chemicals**, speak to your employer about moving to a different job while you are pregnant. Your employer has an obligation to remove you from any work that may endanger your baby.

Chapter 3

Feeding Your Baby

Good health may begin before birth, but the effort doesn't stop after the baby arrives. Caring for a newborn is a demanding and sometimes difficult task. While the responsibility may occasionally seem overwhelming, there is enormous satisfaction in knowing that the efforts you make now will be starting your child on the road to good lifelong health.

Just as your baby relied upon you for protection in the womb, he will rely upon you for protection outside the womb for some time to come. The first and most important step in providing real protection and maximum health benefits is to breastfeed for as long as possible. As with all of us, at all times of life good health begins with what we eat.

The benefits of breastfeeding

No matter what formula manufacturers claim, no matter how healthy the baby in the magazine ad looks, and no matter how much some would like to believe it, artificial milk cannot provide anywhere near the full range of short- and long-term advantages which breast milk does.

Breastfeeding provides all your baby's nutritional needs for up to the first six months of his life. As a newborn's digestive and immune system are still immature, continuous breastfeeding helps prevent food allergies, eczema, asthma and hay fever. Breast milk is economical, always the right temperature and always 'on tap', and while you are breastfeeding your baby you are providing, among other things:

- **Good bacteria** – bifidus growth factor is a helpful organism that guards against intestinal infection by discouraging the growth of yeast, bacteria and parasites in the intestinal tract. Bifidus cannot grow in the intestines of formula-fed babies.
- **Essential fatty acids** – necessary for proper brain development and useful for killing off parasites such as Giardia lamblia, a common cause of diarrhoea in infants.
- **Antioxidants** – breast milk contains the full range to help your baby fight off infection and the effects of pollution. Breast milk is also high in nutrients such as zinc, selenium and taurine (all essential for growth, immunity and proper nerve function) as well as immunity-boosting chemicals such as immunoglobulins and interferon.
- **Immunity** – to several diseases that babies are routinely vaccinated against including measles, mumps and rubella, as well as reduce the risk of Hib disease and maybe pneumococcal diseases. It also protects against chicken pox, respiratory and gastrointestinal infections.
- **A better chance of survival** for low-birth-weight and premature babies.
- **Reduced risk of gastrointestinal infections** such as diarrhoea, as well as protection against other illnesses such as intestinal tract infections, ear infections, colic and food allergies.
- **The building blocks for better intelligence**. A recent Canadian study involving 14,000 children found that exclusive breastfeeding for the first three months of life – or longer – meant that children scored around six points higher in IQ tests by age 6. This squares with data from an earlier large analysis of 20 published studies which found a similar boost in IQ which it concluded was derived from the unique combination of better nutrition and maternal bonding which comes from breastfeeding. Enhanced intelligence was seen in babies as early as 6 months old and was sustained until

15 years of age. The longer a baby was breastfed, the greater the increase in cognitive developmental benefit. Breastfed babies also show better visual development, language and social skills. Switching the baby from one breast to another can help develop better hand–eye coordination.

- **Natural birth control**. This method of birth control is known as the lactational amenorrhea method (LAM). To be effective it must meet three criteria: 1) Your baby must be 6 months of age or younger. After your baby is 6 months old, you are much more likely to become pregnant and need to use another method of birth control to prevent pregnancy; 2) You must fully breastfeed your infant, in an unrestricted way, meaning that the baby receives only breast milk, both day and night feeding, with no long intervals between feedings; and 3) You must not have a period (amenorrhea). When your periods start, use an additional birth-control method. When these conditions are met, LAM has been shown to be 98.5 per cent effective. Even so, many doctors still recommend that couples use another method of birth control.

Full-time breastfeeding burns about 250 calories a day – the equivalent of a three-mile run

A woman's body makes milk according to the baby's demand. If you give your baby fluids and other foods this will decrease the baby's demands on you and thus your milk supply.

The colostrum and milk which a mother makes is all her baby needs for the first 6–7 months of life. Breast milk contains two distinct kinds of liquids. The foremilk, which is more watery and thirst quenching, and the hindmilk which is rich in fats and nutrients. Some women feel bewildered by the concept of two kinds of milk and wonder how on earth they can possibly know if their baby has got both in any one feed. If you follow traditional advice, as pregnancy and birth expert Janet Balaskas, founder of the Active Birth Movement says, and 'feed like a gypsy' (in other words as and when your baby demands) you can't go wrong. Your baby will naturally feed until she has had all she needs.

LIFTING THE LID

There is no such thing as Insufficient Milk Syndrome – formula manufacturers dreamed up this advertising concept more than 20 years ago to boost sales. The vast majority of mothers (more than 90 per cent) can breastfeed without problems.

Breastfeeding mothers shouldn't allow themselves to be encouraged towards early weaning by doctors' 'growth charts'. These are often used to persuade women that their breastfed babies are not growing well. Standard growth charts are only appropriate for bottle-fed babies who tend to gain weight more quickly than breastfed babies. As long as your breastfed baby is putting on weight steadily you can be confident you are following the right course.

Breastfeeding in a toxic world

There has been a great deal in the media recently about toxins in breast milk. Women who are considering breastfeeding their children have rightly expressed concern that the benefits of breast milk may be negated by the presence of harmful chemical such as dioxins and PCBs.

According to a WHO survey, the 'safe' daily intake of dioxins and PCBs is around 10 picograms (pg) per kg of bodyweight. Among breastfed infants the daily estimated intake of these chemicals is around 170pg per kg of body weight at two months and 39pg at 10 months.

So how can we know that breast milk is safe? Thankfully this is an area which has been thoroughly studied, the conclusion being that while prenatal exposure to these levels of toxins has a definite negative effect on a baby's health and development, exposure via breast milk did not have the same dramatic effect.

This does not mean that the issue of contaminated breast milk is not serious, it is. But along with contaminants, breast milk has constituents which help fight toxic overload. The overwhelming opinion of paediatricians and child health experts is that the benefits of breastfeeding still far outweigh the potential risk of ingesting chemicals.

Remember also that a baby formula made with conventional tap water is likely to contain many harmful chemicals and heavy metals without conferring even a minute proportion of the benefits which breast milk has.

However, if you are still worried here are some things you can do to keep toxins out of your breast milk:

- **Adopt an organic lifestyle**. If you don't have pesticides in your body they cannot be transferred to your baby via your breast milk.
- **Reduce your exposure to common household pollutants** such as cleaners, disinfectants and toiletries. Remember that many products we associate with being 'clean' can in fact be full of dangerously toxic chemicals which can be inhaled and quickly absorbed through your skin. When you can't avoid using conventional household cleaners, always wear rubber gloves and open a window to minimise exposure.
- **Don't diet or fast while breastfeeding**. Most toxic chemicals are stored in fat. These poisons are released in great numbers when you begin to lose fat and can accumulate in your bloodstream and breast milk. Full-time breastfeeding burns about 250 calories a day – the equivalent of a three-mile run. Furthermore, according to child health experts the longer a woman breastfeeds, the less contaminated her milk can become. Breastfeeding uses up calories (i.e. burns up fat) and as toxic fat is burned up, this is replaced by non-toxic fat (see below). Following an organic diet will help this process enormously.
- **Work some regular physical activity into your schedule**. Some form of aerobic exercise can aid the release of toxins (via sweat) from your system. Another good way to rid your body of toxins is through regular deep breathing used in yoga and some forms of meditation.
- **Remember, everything you put in your body will get into your breast milk**. So limit or avoid casual use of medicines, caffeine, alcohol and foods with additives such as colourings, aromas, flavourings, MSG and aspartame. Each of these can have a dramatic effect on your baby's developing immune system.

- **Once a week have a soak in a bath with Epsom salts**. This old-fashioned remedy for aches and pains is also good for gently encouraging the release of toxins through the skin. Add a few drops of essential oils for a really pleasant bathtime.

If you choose to bottle-feed

In spite of the overwhelming benefits of breastfeeding, some women still use bottles. While it may sound harsh to equate artificial milk with junk food, that is largely what it is. Investigative journalist Morgan Spurlock dramatically revealed what happens to the body on a biochemical level when it exists solely on a diet of fast food, in his shocking documentary *Fast Food Nation*. In the same way that people who exist on a diet of fast food are biochemically different than those who eat fresh whole food, infants who are fed artificially have been shown to be biochemically different from those who are breastfed. For instance:

- Their blood carries a different pattern of amino acids, some of which may be at levels high enough to cause health concerns. In addition, their blood has a totally different chemical composition, which includes higher levels of urea and electrolytes.
- The composition of their body fat is different. They are fed a variety of carbohydrates to which no other mammalian species is exposed in neonatal life.
- Their guts are colonised from an early age by a potentially invasive type of micro flora that can cause persistent gastrointestinal problems.
- They are exposed to large amounts of foreign protein. Studies have shown that these infants have sometimes overactive immune systems which are continually producing antibodies to these foreign proteins.
- They are also deprived of the immune factors present in human milk, thus they are more vulnerable to natural pathogens in the environment.

Several formula companies now produce organic infant formulas, as well as those based on soya or almonds. While these are most appropriate as follow-on milk once you have stopped breastfeeding, or for mixed feeding after a few months of breastfeeding, they can also be useful for women who cannot or will not breastfeed.

Nevertheless, none of these supplies complete nutrition in itself. Some paediatricians have also noted that rates of eczema can rise with cow's milk formula, the rate of asthma can rise with soya formula, and more frequent diarrhoea has been observed in babies taking almond milk formula. If you are using these types of formulas you might consider rotating them so that your child is not exposed to any one type for too long. This will reduce the risk of an allergic or intolerance reaction.

There are other ways to make bottlefeeding safer:

- **Use an organic formula**. This will reduce your baby's exposure to contaminants present in conventional formulas.
- **Avoid formulas that contain added sugars or glucose**. These sugars (often listed on the label as lactose, maltose, sucrose, maltodextrins, glucose syrup or dried glucose syrup, and pre-cooked starch) can suppress immune function.
- **Make up formula as you need it**, rather than storing large quantities in the fridge. This helps to avoid food-borne bacteria as well as the slow leaking of plasticisers into the formula.
- **Do not heat plastic bottles in boiling w**ater to heat the formula. When heated, the plastic in baby bottles can give off bisphenol-A (BPA) a hormone-disrupting chemical, and plasticisers that can contaminate the formula. Instead, warm the formula separately in a pan, or by making up with cooled boiled water in a separate glass jug, which you then pour into the bottle. Sterilising plastic bottles in boiling water also causes harmful phthalates to migrate from the bottle to the formula. Since older bottles release the most bisphenol-A, a recent report by the WWF recommends changing to new bottles every 6 months.
- **Consider switching to tempered glass bottles**, which are unbreakable and completely free from harmful plasticisers and other toxins. As concern over bisphenol-A has increased, manufacturers are starting to offer BPA-free bottles.

Weaning – when, how and what to feed your baby

A century ago, children weren't given solid foods until they were a year old. Today, solids are being introduced earlier and earlier. Dieticians and paediatricians are divided over the wisdom of this. However, the general consensus is that babies should not have solids until they are 6 to 7 months old. By this time their systems are mature enough to eat mashed foods. Any earlier and the same foods will have to be puréed and strained – more work for mum and a much greater challenge to the immature digestive system of your baby.

AVOIDING FOOD ALLERGIES

To avoid setting up food allergies, try introducing new foods according to the following guidelines:

6–9 months
- Fresh vegetables (except those belonging to the nightshade family: potato, tomato, aubergine, peppers)
- Fresh fruit (except citrus and strawberries)
- Dried fruit (unsulphured)
- Gluten-free grains (brown rice, millet, quinoa, buckwheat)
- Beans and pulses
- Organic poultry, meat and fish (not shellfish)

9–12 months
- Low gluten grains (oats, rye and barley)
- Corn
- Nightshades
- Soy products
- Finely ground nuts and seeds

12–24 months
- Wheat (bread, pasta, flour)
- Dairy products (whole cows' milk, cheese, yogurt)
- Citrus fruit
- Eggs

24+ months
- Shellfish
- Strawberries

Around this time, your baby is ready for more vitamins and calories than your breast milk can supply. So this is a great time to experiment and help your baby explore and enjoy new tastes and textures.

There are no hard and fast rules about when to stop breastfeeding. Introducing solids, particularly dairy and wheat, too early can set your baby up for food intolerance later in life. Babies' intestines are very porous which means that large food molecules can get into the blood system and cause allergic reactions. So it's best to begin with simple foods. Common signs of food intolerance and allergy include rashes, flushing, runny nose, diarrhoea, colic, eczema, crying, breathing problems and dark rings under the eyes.

In general, you should introduce solids a little at a time, perhaps just one meal a day for a week or so. If your baby spits the food out or drools when fed he is probably not quite ready for solids. Wait a few more weeks and try again – otherwise solid food becomes associated with tension and trauma for him, and mess and more work for you. Never force-feed a baby and never add sugar or honey to foods to appeal to your baby's sweet tooth and trick him into eating.

Food in a jar

Whereas once there was no choice on market shelves, or you had to trek to the healthfood shop to buy organic baby foods, today the supermarket shelves are bursting with organic alternatives.

Bottles and jars can be useful supplements to a diet based on home-cooked foods, but no baby should rely solely on pre-packaged foods to fulfil all of his nutritional needs. The best solid food for your baby is food you make yourself. Keeping a little bit of unseasoned food back from your regular meals and putting this through a blender is the cheapest and easiest way to provide nutritious first foods for your baby.

Fresh food has the advantage of supplying important enzymes and amino acids, which are never present in commercially produced foods. From a budgeting point of view, home-made food is also infinitely cheaper, especially if you are giving your baby the same foods (less the seasonings, of course) that you are eating each day.

However, if you have a busy lifestyle or are simply not confident in your ability to cook for your baby, the next best thing is pre-prepared baby foods. Until recently this meant conventional foods which were made from produce sprayed with pesticides and herbicides. Today, however, organic baby foods account for between 15 and 20 per cent of the total baby-food market.

WHAT'S IN THAT JAR?

In 1998 a major US study found that nine out of ten children aged 6 months to 5 years were exposed to 13 different neurotoxic organophosphate pesticides in the food they ate. Many of these children were consuming levels of organophosphates at levels known to cause damage to the developing brain and nervous system.

In this study, conventionally produced baby food including apple juice, apple sauce and meals containing pears and peaches, was one of the main sources of unsafe levels of pesticides.

British researchers have also found multiple pesticide residues in conventional baby food. A 1999 report stated that one in eight baby food jars of regular fruit and vegetable baby meals has pesticide residues in them. Of these, nearly a third contained several pesticides known to cause adverse reproductive effects. The study also concluded that because they only tested a limited range of foods, these results were probably an underestimation and that levels of pesticide residues on produce were probably 20 per cent higher than reported. That same year studies suggested that contamination from the oil in the seal of the lids of baby food jars was a cause for concern. Government tests found toxic contamination from epoxidised soya bean oil (ESBO) in 48 per cent of samples tested.

In 2003, studies showed that a chemical known as semicarbazide (SEM), a potential carcinogen and genotoxin (that is one that can damage DNA), migrated into food from the plastic gaskets used to seal glass jars with metal twist-off lids. Surveys have shown that SEM can be found in both organic and conventional baby foods in significant amounts.

Buying organic

Most concerned parents would reason that as long as they are giving their baby jars of organic food they are giving them the best. Organic baby foods are made of ingredients which have been grown without pesticides, artificial fertilisers and are guaranteed GM-free. Because they are made from organic ingredients they may also be higher in nutrients than conventional baby foods.

But don't buy baby food just because it's organic. All pre-packaged food has drawbacks and health-conscious parents need to become label detectives. For instance, many organic baby foods use fillers such as rice starch and 'natural' sweeteners such as apple or pear juice concentrate to thicken and flavour watered-down foods (and to increase the profit margin).

Equally, a product might trumpet 'no added sugar', but this does not mean that the product is sugar-free. It may contain sugar from other sources such as fruit juice concentrates, and indeed many products which have no added sugar can be just as sugary as those which do not make this claim. The hollow calories in sugars and fillers are a particularly important consideration when choosing food for infants. Because the amount of food a baby can take in is so small, every bite needs to be nutrient-packed.

Apart from fillers and sugars, organic foods may not live up to your expectations in other ways. For instance, the jar may not actually contain much of the nutritious food advertised on the label. A recent report by the Consumers Association in the UK highlighted the fact that everything – even the name of a product – gives a clue to what is really in it. For example a lamb and potato hotpot will have a minimum of 10 per cent lamb in it. But a potato and lamb hotpot can contain less than 10 per cent meat.

Equally, it is wise not to get too caught up in 'healthy choice' claims on the label either, since there are strict laws governing what can and cannot be put into baby foods. For instance, baby foods which claim 'no artificial colours' and 'no preservatives' are not, as you might think, doing your baby a big favour. Artificial colours and preservatives are not allowed by law in any baby foods. Likewise, there are rules and recommendations governing the amount of salt and the types of flavourings allowed in baby foods.

WHAT IS ORGANIC?

Where organic baby foods are concerned, a product may be certified organic if it contains at least 95 per cent organic ingredients. This allows for the fact that some things, such as vitamins used to fortify the foods, cannot be found in an organic form. Parents concerned about what might be in that other 5 per cent should read labels carefully and make the decision whether to purchase based on what they find.

Think also about the claim 'added vitamins and minerals'. Food manufacturers often add vitamins and minerals, to nutritionally poor foods that have lost their nutrients during processing. This is not always a bad thing, though; fortified foods that contain extra iron can be useful for those babies who do not eat meat.

Simple ideas for first foods

Early foods should consist of fruits, cereal and vegetables (introducing protein comes later). It is best to introduce new foods one at a time, so give your baby a large amount of one single food at meal time rather than lots of little tastes of lots of foods. Doing this assures that your baby does not develop an allergic reaction to food. Strange as it seems, small amounts of new foods are more likely to cause an allergic reaction than a larger amount.

In general, if a food can be eaten raw such as banana, avocado pear, papaya or a very ripe pear, then give it raw. Mashing these foods or putting them through a sieve or a mouli (a small food grinder ideal for making baby foods) as and when you need them, will ensure that you baby is getting the most vitamins, minerals enzymes and fibre from that product. But some first foods will have to be cooked. It is very important that you do not use seasonings such as salt and pepper or butter when cooking baby foods. A young baby's systems cannot handle these yet.

While some parents choose to introduce baby drinks – for instance baby juices – early on, these are not necessary and even if you make them yourself from diluted fruit juice they are not as good for your baby as water (and, for infants, breast milk). Despite the manufacturers'

IRON-RICH FOODS

Early foods should be rich in iron since after about 6 months of breastfeeding your baby's stores will begin to run low. Iron-rich foods include:

- Whole lentils
- Green leafy vegetables such as broccoli, green cabbage, spinach, kale, watercress, parsley and peas
- Crude blackstrap molasses
- Wholegrains such as millet and amaranth
- Iron-fortified rice or oat cereals (no wheat)

hype, baby juices, even organic ones, are simply too sugary to be healthy and it is best to get your baby in the habit of drinking water to quench his thirst early on. Some parents switch from breast milk to a follow-on formula, which may be healthier over the short term than putting a baby directly onto cows' milk. An infant's ability to digest cows' milk properly is poor and introducing it before your baby is a year old can lead to allergy and intolerance. If you choose to include a follow-on formula in your baby's diet, choose the organic option, but always compare labels for things like sugar content, which can vary enormously between brands.

As your baby gets older, and hungrier, healthy snacks of fresh fruit and things like breadsticks, rice cakes, toast or plain pasta are acceptable.

Below are some suggestions for easy-to-make first foods. The best way to make cooked foods is to make them in quantity and freeze them in ice-cube trays. Trial and error will show you how much to feed your baby but as a general rule of thumb, at 6 months or so two cubes will make an adequate meal for most babies.

Simple apple purée
Apples are rich in vitamin C.
1kg (2lb) of organic eating apples, peeled and cored
250ml (9floz) filtered water

Put the apples and water in a pan and bring to the boil, then simmer until the fruit is soft. When cooled, purée in a blender to the desired consistency. Pour the mixture into ice-cube trays and freeze for use later.

To add a little extra flavour you can add a scant pinch of cinnamon to the recipe while you are cooking.

This purée can be added to rice cereal to make a creamy and slightly sweet breakfast cereal.

Three fruit purée

A nice little treat for your baby that is rich in essential nutrients. Make it as you need it since bananas don't freeze that well.

If you have made your apple purée ahead of time you can simply mix this with a very ripe mashed pear and a little banana. Process these through a mouli or through a sieve and serve.

White fish and spinach main meal

White fish such as pollock or cod has a mild flavour, is high in protein and a good first taste of seafood.

1 cod fillet
2 handfuls of spinach
100ml (4floz) filtered water
50g (2floz) brown rice, well cooked

Steam or oven cook the cod and spinach. Put in a food processor with the rice and blend to the desired consistency.

Baby oatmeal

For a simple creamed cereal suitable for babies aged 9–12 months, start with organic oats. These can be ground up in blender or coffee grinder until they are a fine powder and stored in an airtight container, or just ground and used as needed.

Mix this with a warm liquid made up of roughly equal amounts of oats and water, or even better, breast milk). Stir into a smooth gruel.

Oats are naturally sweet and rich in iron so you do not need to add anything else.

Purée of courgette and potato with watercress

Any vegetable can be made into a delicious purée. Since potato is a member of the nightshade family it is best suited to babies aged 9–12 months. Courgette (zucchini) and watercress are iron-rich foods.

1 large organic potato (peeled and chopped)
1 medium courgette (washed, unpeeled)
a small handful of chopped watercress leaves
a little water or breast milk

Steam the potato until nearly tender. Add the courgette and watercress and cook until completely tender.

The cooked mixture can then be puréed using water or breast milk to adjust the consistency.

Butternut squash purée

This subtly flavoured orange squash is similar to pumpkin. It is rich in beta-carotene. All you need is one butternut squash.

Cut the squash in half, then peel and remove the seeds. Cut the flesh up into small cubes and steam for 8 to 10 minutes until soft. Purée in a food processor or mouli. Use water, breast milk or formula to adjust the consistency. You can freeze the mixture in ice-cube trays for future use.

THE NUTRIENTS YOU CAN'T SEE

One reason why weaning can be difficult is that it does not provide the same feeling of intimacy as breastfeeding. Sharing, intimacy and love are important nutrients which help your child grow.

Just like a stressed-out adult, a stressed-out child is less able to absorb nutrients from food and is more prone to attacks from toxins in the environment. Keeping these new-style mealtimes calm and happy means your baby will learn to enjoy solids and will also be getting all the necessary nutrients from them.

Chapter 4

Keeping Your Baby Clean

Babies can be messy; they need to be cleaned and changed more or less constantly for many months after birth. It's a parental certainty that the first time you put your baby into a cute outfit you've just bought, she will spit up over the front of it or produce a spectacular bowel movement that no nappy could possibly contain!

Because babies need frequent cleaning and changing, and because nappies, in particular, sit so close to the skin, it is worth learning more about what they are comprised of. Likewise, all those baby products we use to clean and moisturise a baby's skin may not be as simple or as benign – or even as necessary – as they appear.

As with all aspects of 'green' living, the key to green parenting is to be well informed and to simplify wherever possible.

Keeping your baby dry

Nappies. It's not a subject which is guaranteed to have all eyes riveted on you at a dinner party (except possibly in pity). You may never see anyone choose it as their specialist subject in a TV quiz; in fact, there are many who would just as well not think about nappies or their contents at all. Babies as we all know from TV, magazines and films are supposed to gurgle and coo, not poop and fart (this in spite of the fact that the average baby will require 5,000 nappy changes before his third birthday).

Nevertheless, there are important changes going on in the world of nappies. The concept of 'real' nappies – that is reusable, cloth nappies – is becoming more and more accepted by parents as a genuine alternative to lugging home mega packs of what amount to bin liners for little bottoms.

Disposable nappies contain up to 200 synthetic chemicals

When disposable nappies first came out they seemed like a god-send to may parents. Mothers in their thousands said goodbye to washing soiled clothes and instead just dumped the new-style nappies in the bin with all the other household waste. Years later, the bad news about disposable nappies began to emerge. Scientists and ecologists informed us that disposables were not really disposable after all.

Instead, they take thousands of years to biodegrade which means that every soiled nappy that was ever thrown away is still festering somewhere under the earth.

Disposable nappies are a relatively new invention – within the last 30 years or so – and the technology behind them has evolved tremendously in the last decade. Studies suggest they may contain up to 200 synthetic chemicals; it is still unknown how many are absorbed through a baby's skin. Most modern disposables contain a 'chemical sponge' – an absorbent gelling material – called sodium polyacrylate. This super-absorbent gel, which can soak up 30 times its own weight in liquid, emits an oestrogen-like chemical which has the potential to damage a young boy's fertility when kept in constant close contact with the testicles. Similarly, a study in 2000 found that disposable nappies keep babies' testicles at higher-than-normal temperatures, which may also affect future fertility.

This may sound shocking, yet we know that sperm counts are declining throughout the developed world and medical scientists are at a loss to explain exactly why. Chances are it's a combination of different influences, but disposables cannot be ruled out as one cause of sexual dysfunction later in life. Super-absorbent gel when dry is a powder and paediatricians report that it can travel up the urogenital tract of boys and into the vaginas of little girls, where it may cause damage and scarring.

LIFTING THE LID

The 3 billion disposable nappies thrown away each year add 1 million tonnes of nappy waste to our already overfull landfill sites. They then take up to 500 years to decompose, and produce the potent greenhouse gas methane and leachate, a toxic liquid that can leak into soil and local water supplies. The 10 per cent that aren't sent to landfill get incinerated, a process that results in the release of carcinogenic dioxins into the atmosphere and creates ash (which then needs to be sent to landfill) containing heavy metals and other toxins.

It took a while for news like this to settle in, but slowly there has been a change in consciousness among many parents. Perhaps not surprisingly, the trend for using cotton nappies has taken off in the last few years, particularly as parents have become more eco-conscious. There are now a great many companies supplying baby-shaped cotton nappies with Velcro fastenings and plastic inner linings which are just as absorbent and a great deal kinder to your baby's skin.

Several companies now produce cotton or cotton/polyester mix nappies, usually with Velcro fasteners. Some produce plastic or woollen outer pants, silk liners and super absorbent cotton boosters for night time use. Once you have a baby you will be doing a load of laundry every day any way, and including nappies in the wash may actually work out cheaper than using disposables.

While some parents fear they may have to change reusable nappies more often than disposables, this is not true. Regardless of whether you are using washables or disposables, young babies need to be changed frequently as their skin is very sensitive to prolonged contact with faeces, urine, creams and powders. Paediatricians recommend new babies be changed 10–12 times a day, and older babies six times. A good-quality cotton nappy should only need changing every four hours during the day and every won't require changing during the night.

TRY A NAPPY SERVICE

If you can't bear the thought of washing them yourself, consider a nappy service. Nappy services are a growing and genuinely practical alternative, especially for mothers who are busy with work or caring for more than one child.

Nappy services can provide parents with freshly laundered, reusable nappies and collect soiled ones, for roughly the same price as the purchase of disposables. See the resources section for more information

Contrary to popular belief, you do not have to boil nappies to disinfect them. A 60°C wash is perfectly adequate to clean and sterilise nappies. Unless you are terribly squeamish, you do not need to wash nappies separately from other clothes. Otherwise, if you have a short, fast or 'eco' facility of your machine, use it. It's the temperature, not the number of rinses which is important. Sunlight can be the best way to bleach cotton nappies.

Disposable-nappy manufacturers may promote the fact that their nappies absorb more moisture, but a baby is not uncomfortable in a moist nappy. It is only when the nappy is left on too long that it will make the skin sore. In fact, there are two significant benefits to this feeling of moistness. First of all, the baby learns the basic sensations that will help it to potty train. Second, the carer knows whether the baby is drinking enough, which is incredibly important if your baby has a fever and is in danger of becoming dehydrated.

It is also a myth that reusable nappies leak. If they fit properly, a reusable nappy is no more likely to leak than an average disposable. In fact, a well-fitting reusable will give even better protection than a disposable nappy.

Disposables are still useful for emergencies and for travel, and some parents may prefer them at night time. Even better, today there are some varieties which are made from organic constituents that are truly biodegradable, and which do not have the highly suspect super-absorbent gels in them.

Nevertheless, there are several advantages to using nappies made from natural fibres. For example:

- **Economy**. Washed carefully, as you would any other item of clothing, cotton nappies should last you through two (or more!) children. Cloth nappies can be washed and reused up to 200 times and then retired into lint-free rags.
- **Less nappy rash**. The absorbent material in disposables can make a nappy feel dry even when it is wet. Parents may be tempted to leave the baby in the nappy for longer, exposing the baby to the ammonia which urine produces as it breaks down. This ammonia can irritate the skin and produce nappy rash.
- **No suspect chemicals**. Conventional nappies are bleached using chlorine bleach. Because of this they can off-gas dioxins – a carcinogenic byproduct of the bleaching process. They also contain a 'chemical sponge', the absorbent gelling material sodium polyacrylate. This gel emits an oestrogen-like chemical with the potential to reduce future fertility when kept in constant close contact with the testicles. Super-absorbent gel when dry is a powder, and paediatricians report that it can travel up the urogenital tract of boys and into the vaginas of little girls where it may cause damage and scarring.
- **Better use of world resources**. According to the 1996 Women's Environmental Network report *Preventing Nappy Waste*, using cotton nappies ultimately conserves the earth's resources. Based on 5,020 nappy changes over a two-and-a-half-year period they estimate that while both systems require similar amounts of fossil fuel energy to produce, disposables use three-and-a-half-times more total energy, eight times more non-renewable materials and a staggering 90 times more renewable materials. Disposables produce 60 times more solid waste, and use 25 per cent more land for growing the materials used in their manufacture.
- **Less waste**. Every day, in the UK alone, 9 million disposable nappies are tipped into landfill sites and it is estimated that nappy waste comprises 4 per cent of all household waste. At least 100 viruses found in faeces can survive for over two weeks in rubbish. Run-off from a landfill site containing such viruses can contaminate groundwater supplies.

ECO-DISPOSABLES

Some people choose to use 'eco-disposable' nappies, believing them to be better for the environment. Eco-disposables are a viable alternative to conventional disposables when you are travelling and at other times when reusables really aren't practical. They are unbleached, use less plastics and chemicals, and therefore expose babies to fewer synthetic materials. And, theoretically, they are biodegradable. However, eco-disposable nappies do go to landfill just like any other nappy, and in landfill they don't break down. They are better for the environment than traditional disposables, but they still contribute to the waste problem.

Many parents groan at the idea of using cloth nappies. They recoil at the inconvenience of having to shake solids into the toilet. They visualise piles of soiled nappies which will keep them chained to the washing machine day in, day out, and the old-fashioned spectre of having to boil pans of nappies to get them germ-free hangs over their heads. Yet as more and more parents are finding out, none of these images reflect the reality of reusables today. In fact, according to a recent consumer survey, usage of washable nappies has risen by 6 per cent in the last couple of years as more and more parents discover that nappies really are changing.

Keeping your baby clean
Baby bath, baby oil, baby lotion, baby wipes. A quick skim of supermarket or pharmacy shelves and you could be forgiven for thinking that having a baby was more of an opportunity for niche shopping than a responsibility towards the future.

Baby toiletries are not significantly different from adults ones. They are largely made from petrochemically derived and synthetic ingredients. Parents looking to keep their babies safe from toxic chemicals might be shocked at just how many unique chemicals they expose their children to each day just by bathing them and applying moisturisers.

Skin, the largest organ of the body, is both a crucial physical barrier and a significant route of absorption of toxic substances. Children's skin is thinner and more absorbent than that of adults, so it provides a less effective barrier to environmental toxins. In addition, the fact that children are smaller in size means that their skin presents a larger surface area relative to their body weight for absorption of harmful substances.

In the developed world, the rate of eczema and allergies among children is on the rise. The early introduction of harsh toiletries onto sensitive skin may be a contributing factor. Unfortunately, parents whose children have skin rashes often approach the problem by piling on more synthetic gloop, when cutting out baby toiletries entirely would be a more rational and effective solution.

There is ample reason to consider the bigger picture of our use of baby toiletries and question whether all those three-for-twos that parents stock up on are really the bargains they appear to be.

Baby bath and wipes

Of all the available bath products, bubble baths, which are highly fragranced, have the greatest potential to cause skin irritation, allergic skin reactions and headaches.

CARING FOR SENSITIVE SKIN

You don't need soap to have a wash. If your skin is very dry or irritated try making your own herbal wash bag. Cut the foot off an old pair of tights, about 15cm (6in) from the end. Fill the pouch with a handful of oatmeal, some soothing herbs such as camomile or lavender and 30ml (2tbsp) of finely ground almonds. Tie a knot in the open end of the pouch. You can now use this in the bath or shower. One wash bag will last one day maximum – keep it in the fridge in a plastic bag if you intend to use it morning and night, but don't try to store it longer than this as it can accumulate bacteria. When wet, it will produce a lovely creamy liquid that will clean and nourish your skin without drying it. This is great for babies, children and adults with dry skin.

A NICE CLEAN BABY

Newborn babies are not 'dirty'. The amount of vernix (the white waxy substance that protect babies' skin whilst in the watery environment of the womb) and/or blood, which covers a newborn baby varies enormously. It is probably fair to say that it is not babies, but midwives, doctors and parents who prefer the smell of talcum powder and cream. Today, the view is that vernix acts to protect the newborn's sensitive skin during the first days of life and should be left to come off naturally over a period of time.

However, a bigger problem with using bubble baths is that they can irritate more than just your skin. Regular bubble bath-use is associated with a high rate of urinary tract infections. The harsh detergents in these products can strip away protective oils from sensitive areas of skin as well as stripping away the mucous which lines the genito-urinary tract. Removing this natural protection allows bacteria to take hold. Children are particularly vulnerable and bubble baths are a major cause of urogenital infections in babies.

As an alternative to a proper wash, the convenience of wipes is such that in the last decade there has been an unprecedented boom in the use of disposable cloths of all kinds. Today in any supermarket, along with the ubiquitous baby wipes, you can buy hand wipes, self-tan and deodorant wipes, make-up- and nail-polish-removing, blackhead-clearing, car washing, multi-surface, disinfecting, furniture, floor, fridge and hob wipes.

Made from plastic, cellulose and polyester fibres pressed together and soaked in a cleaning fluid, even people who don't have babies can often be seen buying packets of baby wipes to use as instant clean-ups anywhere.

Figures from the US suggest that if someone were to load all the disposable wipes purchased there in 2006 onto 18-wheel lorries, the caravan would number 9,000 trucks, stretch for 68 miles, and would be carrying 83,000 tons of used convenience cloths.

Apart from catering to our throwaway society, wipes have other disadvantages; they are expensive, can't be flushed down the toilet and clog sewer systems when they are (even so, few manufacturers include information on 'flushability' on their packets). They are also very slow to biodegrade. As is the case with disposable nappies, it is likely that all the wipes we've ever used are still festering somewhere under the ground. The environmental impact of this has never been studied.

Using fragrance-free products goes part of the way towards reducing your child's risk of exposure

Furthermore, packs of wipes are the prefect breeding ground for germs. To counteract this, wipes manufacturers add large amounts of preservatives and antibacterials. What happens to these chemicals when they enter the waste system has never been studied. On human skin they can be irritating, break down the skin's own protective barrier and cause sensitisation and dermatitis. While they are intended for use only on this skin, some of the chemicals in wipes can be transferred to foods during preparation and into your body when you eat.

Talcum powder

Talcum powder is a traditional mainstay of freshness. We use it liberally on babies' bottoms and to absorb perspiration on hot summer days and nights. A few of us are old enough to remember our mothers having special dishes of talc in the bathroom which had big inviting powder puffs to help you dust your body, and most of the bathroom floor, with the stuff.

But time marches on, and the romantic illusion of talc has taken a huge knock. Talc (magnesium silicate) is made up of finely ground particles of stone. As it originates in the ground, and is a mined product, it can be contaminated with other substances such as asbestos. Recent reports about the talc used in crayon manufacture being contaminated with this poisonous substance have cause alarm to every parent whose child has ever sucked a crayon.

The harmful effects of talc on human tissue were first recorded in

TRY THIS INSTEAD

Let common sense prevail when it comes to keeping your baby clean. Not all babies enjoy early baths and not all parents find bathing their newborn the relaxing scene it is often made out to be. So why not give yourselves a break. If you want to wash your baby, consider the 'top and tail' approach, rinsing the bottom area and face only, with plain water for the first few weeks or more. Remember these golden rules:

- **Use less.** A newborn baby is many times more likely to absorb toxic substances from a toiletry product that an adult, so use sparingly.
- **Look beyond the hype.** Even those baby bath products that are extra mild will be too harsh for most babies. Many paediatricians have expressed concern for babies who are exposed to detergents, creams and oils at a time when their skin is so thin and permeable. Skin reactions to liquid and bar soaps are common and bubble baths, which strip the skin and mucous membranes of protective oils, are a major cause of urogenital infections in newborns and infants.
- **Always opt for vegetable and glycerine-based soaps** over harsher petrochemical-based varieties.
- **Buy real soap** made from at least 70 per cent vegetable oil. Many health food shops stock such soaps or you can order them from specialist suppliers.
- **Choose a liquid castile soap** instead of a body wash. Liquid castile soaps (such as those made by Dr Bronner) foam beautifully and are made from enriching oils such as coconut, hemp and olive. They are usually (but check the label) fragranced with essential oils and even come unscented so you can add your own fragrance.
- **Go fragrance-free.** Fragrances used in room fresheners, soaps, deodorants, baby wipes and lotions, and cleaning agents all contain highly volatile fragrance compounds which have been shown to be carcinogenic and allergenic, capable of altering central nervous system (CNS) function and depressing immune system function. Using fragrance-free products goes part of the way towards reducing your child's risk of exposure.

Ctd

- **Baby wipes can contain alcohol** that can irritate your baby's skin. Plain water is all that is necessary to clean your baby during nappy changes. Use cotton wool for smaller babies, and tissue followed by a wash cloth for older babies. Wipes can be useful if you are travelling or in situations where you are otherwise pressed for time. But because they are slow to biodegrade, keep their use to a minimum, and opt for organic brands that are free from alcohol and fragrances.

the 1930s. More recently a report from the US National Toxicology Program concluded that talc is carcinogenic.

An ominous series of studies has linked talc to ovarian cancer; in them talc was observed in a number of ovarian and uterine tumours as well as in ovarian tissue. It has since been confirmed that talc, either placed directly on the perineum or on the surface of underwear or sanitary towels, can reach the ovaries via ascent through the Fallopian tubes. It is now estimated that women who frequently use talc have three times the risk of developing ovarian cancer compared to non-users.

Talc is mined from the ground and so can be contaminated with substances like asbestos

The talc used in the manufacture of condoms carries a similar risk. In the 1960s the medical journal *The Lancet* reported the first case of a woman who had a significant amount of talc in her peritoneal (abdominal) cavity. Laboratory tests confirmed that the talc in her body matched that found on the surface of her husband's condoms. The authors concluded that the talc travelled up through the Fallopian tubes and became implanted in her abdomen. Talc sprinkled on diaphragms may also be implicated in such problems.

Talc use is also associated with respiratory problems. Because it is comprised of finely ground stone it can lodge in the lungs and never leave. Babies whose mothers smother them in talc have more breathing difficulties and/or urogenital problems. Women are also at risk since even if they don't use talcum powder on their bodies, they are likely to be using cosmetics (powders, eyeshadows, blushers) that are talc-based.

TRY THIS INSTEAD

Talcum powder and cream can actually make your baby dirtier. It can become sticky and unpleasant if your baby becomes overheated, hot and sweaty. Inhaling talcum powder, which can be contaminated with asbestos, is a cause of respiratory problems in babies. Giving up body powders is relatively easy. Giving up your eye shadow may be less so (try applying it with a damp sponge to minimise fallout). But whatever you can do to cut your exposure to talc will benefit your health.

- **Make your own.** You can quickly and easily make a very efficient and inexpensive body powder based on cornstarch. Combine one part bicarbonate of soda to eight parts cornstarch. Mix these up in a coffee grinder or blender and add 10–15 drops of your favourite essential oil (optional). Store in an airtight container (either a jar or an old talc container, or you can recycle a Parmesan cheese shaker).
- **Babies' bottoms do not need talc** or any other powder to stay fresh. Instead, let your baby go without nappies as often as possible, or investigate cotton nappies which allow the skin to breathe and have been shown to cause less nappy rash than disposables.

If you still want to use powder, choose from natural cornstarch-based products which work well to absorb moisture but carry none of the risk factors of talc.

Lotions and creams

Commonly used baby lotions can make the skin feel soft at first, but over time they can actually make babies' skin more dry and more permeable, allowing other toxic ingredients to be absorbed into the body. There is also some evidence that moisturisers can make the skin more susceptible to damage caused by the synthetic detergents used in many baby wash products.

While body oil may seem like a more straightforward alternative to complicated cream or lotion mixtures, many are based on mineral oil (paraffinum liquidum). Some, like baby oil, are 100 per cent mineral oil with added perfume.

Mineral oil, a by-product of the distillation of gasoline from crude oil, impedes the skin's ability to breathe, attract moisture and detoxify. It can also slow down cell renewal and promote premature skin ageing. While it is used for its lubricant qualities which in the short-term appear to make the skin softer, used over the longer-term mineral oil can make the skin dry out. This is because mineral oil dissolves the skin's natural oils, thereby increasing water loss (dehydration) from the skin.

Any mineral oil-derivative can be contaminated with cancer-causing polycyclic aromatic hydrocarbons (PAHs). Mineral oils may also increase the skin's sensitivity to sunlight and have been linked to an increased risk of skin cancer. Petrolatum, paraffin or paraffin oil and propylene glycol are all forms of mineral oil, so look out for these in the ingredients of products you are considering adding to your shopping trolley.

Among women who switch toiletry brands or try new products, mineral oils have been shown to the major cause of new skin irritation including rashes and spots. There is no good reason for this kind of suffering. Because of the risks of mineral oils, some manufacturers have switched to using silicone-based oils and gels.

Silicones such as dimethicone (or dimethiconol), cyclomethicone, cyclopentasiloxane and cyclohexasiloxane are synthesised from silicon metal to produce water repellent 'dry' oils and waxes. They add many of the feel-good qualities associated with modern body-care products such as texture, silkiness, lustre and smooth application.

On the whole, silicones allow the skin to breathe better than mineral oils but question marks still hang over their long-term safety. Some, like dimethicone, are also cancer suspects.

TRY THIS INSTEAD

If you are breastfeeding, your baby is less likely to suffer from nappy rash since breast milk is well metabolised by the baby's digestive system, which means that waste products such as urine and faeces are less likely to contain skin-irritating substances. Unless your baby has an underlying skin condition that requires medical attention, she probably doesn't need a regular moisturiser applied to the nappy area.

- **Mineral oil** does not moisturise the skin. It puts a sticky barrier on top of it that can trap dirt, prevent the skin breathing and will eventually strip essential moisture from it.
- **Use natural oils.** Effective moisturisers can be prepared on an 'as needed' basis by almost anyone from a simple mixture of vegetable or biological oils, such as coconut, jojoba, almond or emu (emu oil is an animal oil produced as a by product of emu meat production – it is particulary good for dry skin) and plant 'butters' (shea or mango), water and glycerine. With practice you will find the one that suits your baby's needs. The advantage of natural oils is that they contain all the nutrients natural to the plant, or animal. Many such as jojoba and emu are amazingly similar to the oils in human skin and as such are non-irritating, don't clog pores and are deeply nourishing.
- **Choose organic products** with the fewest ingredients. It is the oil and wax content of moisturisers that holds moisture next to the skin, so why not consider simple vegetable oils to maintain the skin's suppleness. They will do the same job at a fraction of the price and you'll have the advantage of actually knowing what you are putting on your baby's skin. As a general rule, use lighter oils such as apricot kernel, coconut or jojoba oil for normal skins, and heavier oils such as avocado and evening primrose oil for drier skins. Rosehip oil is also considered a rich and nourishing oil for dry or irritated skin.
- **To avoid nappy rash and dry, cracked skin**, let your baby go without a nappy as often as possible. Getting air on to your baby's skin is the best way to keep it healthy.

Sun creams

Exposure to the fresh air and sun is vital for a healthy body. Sunlight, for example, is an important source of vitamin D necessary for development and maintenance of bones and teeth. But at the same time, too much sun exposure is not appropriate for babies (or, for that matter, grown ups).

Relying on sunscreens as your sole means of protection is fraught with problems since the protection they offer is never guaranteed. In addition, most commercial sun creams contain a mixture of harsh and harmful chemicals that present their own risks. For example, some of the chemicals in sunscreens are thought to cause disruption or permanent damage to the nervous, immune and respiratory systems. It is not uncommon for sun creams to contain three or more sunscreen agents as well as perfumes, insect repellents and a host of other chemicals besides. Young children may be especially susceptible to sunscreen chemicals and their toxic side-effects.

There are two basic types of creams available on the market today: chemical sunscreens, which act by absorbing ultraviolet (UV) light, and chemical sunblocks, which reflect or scatter light in both the visible and ultraviolet spectrum. Both types are associated with skin irritation.

These are the most common chemical sunscreens:

- **Benzophenones** are common skin sensitisers and can provoke allergic reactions in some individuals. Common benzophenones include oxybenzone, dioxybenzone and sulisbenzone.
- **PABAs** are formaldehyde-forming chemicals that can form carcinogenic nitrosamines when combined with amines such as DEA, TEA and MEA in the mixture. PABAs can cause skin irritation. Common PABAs are p-aminobenzoic acid, ethyl dihydroxypropyl PABA, padimate-O (ocyl dimethyl PABA), padimate A and glyceryl PABA.
- **Cinnamates** are common skin irritants. This group of chemical includes cinoxate, ethylhexyl-p-methoxycinnamate, octocrylene and ocytl methoxycinnamate.
- **Salicylates** are also skin irritants and are associated with a high rate of dermatitis among users. Those commonly used in sun creams include ethylhexyl salicylate, homosalate, octyl salicylate and neo-homosalate.

- Other common sunscreen agents include methyl anthranilate, digalloyl trioleate and avobenzone (butyl methoxy-dibenzoylmethane).
- The most commonly used chemical sunblocks are: zinc oxide, titanium dioxide and red petrolatum.

The latest controversy in natural sunscreens concerns micro-fine particles of zinc oxide and titanium dioxide. These are of course effective sunblocks that have been used for years. But they tend to leave a whitish sheen on the skin and so manufacturers have turned to nanotechnology to try and solve the problem. Most sunblocks on the market now make use of nanoparticles of zinc oxide and titanium dioxide that in theory are small enough to slip through the upper layers of the skin.

Natural sunscreens

Read the labels on natural and 'organic' sunscreens carefully. Usually they contain simply the same ingredients as conventional products with added plant extracts and oils. Can the addition of these natural ingredients really prevent against sunburn? No, of course not. For example:

- **Aqua** – water does not prevent sunburn.
- **Glycerin** – a lubricant used in moisturisers to make them feel good and go on more smoothly. It has no sun-blocking ability but can dry the skin making it more vulnerable to sun damage.
- **Octyl palmitate** – a relative of vitamin C. There is no evidence it can provide protection from the sun.
- **Retinyl palmitate** – also known as pro-vitamin A or pro-retinol, there is no evidence of sun protection.
- **Tocopherol acetate** – a relative vitamin E. Again, no evidence it has any effect as a sunscreen.
- Other ingredients including aloe vera, carrot oil, camomile, borage oil and avocado oil are used as fillers, stabilisers or preservatives. They are seldom present in high enough quantities to protect or nourish your skin and none of them have proven sun-blocking ability.

TRY THIS INSTEAD

Around 80 per cent of our total lifetime exposure to the sun comes during childhood. So it is especially important to make sure children have some protection from strong sunlight. If you want to teach your children good sun exposure habits, lead by example. Research into children's voluntary use of sun creams, for example, suggests that they copy what their parents do. Consider some simple strategies for enjoying the sun:

- **Don't be afraid of the sun**. Babies need a little daily exposure to sun and fresh air like the rest of us. This does not mean foolishly leaving your child exposed to hours of sunlight but rather enjoying the sun as a natural part of your daily routine. Studies show that we all need approximately 15–20 minutes of sun exposure on our face, arms and legs each day to produce and maintain vital supplies of vitamin D. Staying out of the sun means many of us do not get enough vitamin D and this has led to the re-emergence of diseases like rickets, and contributed to spiralling rates of depression as well as cancers of the breast, prostate and colon.
- **Cover up.** When you and your children are going to be out in the sun for extended periods of time, make practical use of T-shirts, sunglasses, hats and beach umbrellas. It is also worth investigating special UV-protective sunsuits for babies. These have a high SPF and can be useful if you are somewhere very sunny or are for whatever reason out in the sun for an extended period. Remember though that you don't need special clothing to protect you from the sun. Most summer clothes provide an SPF of more than. An average-weight T-shirt provides an SPF of 7. Fabrics dyed black, navy-blue, white, green or beige provide the highest SPF.
- **Limit time in the sun.** It is best to avoid being out when the sun is at its strongest, between the hours of 11am and 2pm.
- **Keep babies under 6 months old out of strong sunlight.** It is a much more effective way of protecting your child than slapping on suncream. Baby sun creams with a high SPF probably have the greatest number of toxic chemicals and are not suitable for the delicate and permeable skin of babies.

While manufacturers say these particles are perfectly safe, no study has yet been done to find out how much more the body absorbs of these nanoscale particles and what the potential health effects might be. In 2006, a US laboratory study found that nanoscale titanium oxide could upset the chemical balance of the brain and produce brain damage. Such results add to a growing body of evidence that suggests that the safety of nanoscale ingredients cannot be taken for granted simply because larger particles of the same substance have no ill effects.

Toothpaste

As soon as your baby's first milk teeth arrive it's important to start to brush them to encourage good dental health. A soft, good-quality brush is a must and to accompany this, most parents will opt for a toothpaste of some kind. But recent evidence suggests that toothpaste is not only unnecessary but contains ingredients that you may not want your baby exposed to.

By far the most controversial ingredient in toothpaste, however, is fluoride. Many of us still buy fluoride-containing toothpastes believing that fluoride protects teeth. There is, however, little convincing scientific evidence of this. Instead, fluoride is a systemic poison. There is enough in the average tube of family toothpaste to kill a small child if ingested. For this reason both the American FDA and the Swedish National Food Administration now require that toothpaste containing fluoride be labelled with a special 'poison' warning.

LIFTING THE LID

It is now widely accepted that family toothpastes which generally have the highest amounts of fluoride in them (around 1500 ppm, or parts per million) are unsuitable for children under the age of eight. If you are going to buy a fluoride toothpaste for your chid, use a children's formula and supervise brushing to make sure it doesn't get swallowed.

Fluoride can cause sensitivity/allergic type reactions and is now suspected in a host of illnesses including gastroesophageal reflux disease (GERD), bone problems, diabetes, thyroid malfunction and mental impairment.

Fluoride exposure from toothpaste, supplements and water before the age of six is also an important risk factor for dental fluorisis, which mottles and discolours the teeth. In addition, young children also have a tendency to swallow toothpaste and with it the potentially poisonous fluoride. This may be because they are too young to control their swallowing or it may simply be that sweet flavours and pretty colours make toothpaste as appealing as confectionery to swallow.

TRY THIS INSTEAD

Try to develop good brushing habits for your children from the appearance of their first tooth. How well baby teeth develop and how healthy they are will be a good indication of how healthy their adult teeth will be.

- **Start brushing early,** as soon as your baby's first tooth pops through. You don't need toothpaste to do this. It is the brushing, not the paste, that keeps baby's teeth clean.
- **If you wish to use toothpaste** look for a natural non-fluoride-containing brand – there are plenty of good options available in health food shops and on the internet. You don't need more than a smear on a small soft brush to clean a baby's teeth.
- **Give your baby a soft toothbrush** to chew on while teething. It can soothe sore gums and helps keep teeth clean.

Chapter 5

Baby's Bedroom

Over the years, many of us have got used to having drawers and closets full of inexpensive clothes that we wear for a season and discard when fashion changes. Manufacturers have given consumers exactly what was demanded: the cheapest possible goods made from the cheapest possible methods – often using dangerous chemicals in the spirit that the end justifies the means.

Consumers' appetite for cheap clothing that can be discarded once it loses it fashion value, however, results in spending with little moral or social accountability. Yet fast clothing, like fast food, has a lot to answer for in terms of its environmental impact and it potential effects on health.

At every step along the way, conventionally produced textiles are treated with and absorb toxic chemicals and these chemicals may also affect the consumers' health during the use of the cloth products.

You may wonder what this has to do with babies. The answer is that babies spend a lot of time wearing sleepsuits, lying in their cots. What they wear and what they sleep on can be continual sources of chemical exposures.

Conventional clothes and bedding are made from a mixture of natural fibres such as cotton which have been sprayed with tonnes of pesticides, and synthetic fabrics which can give off toxic gases. In addition, many children's clothes, especially nightwear, are treated with toxic flame retardant.

For many parents, the switch to simpler, more eco-friendly textiles requires an enormous leap in our perception of risk. And yet if you care about what you put in your baby's body, it's only a matter of time before you have to scrutinise what you put on your baby's body as well.

Cotton is the second most pesticide-dependent crop in the world, accounting for 10 per cent of global pesticide use

The hidden ingredients in clothes

Clothing at its most basic level exists primarily to protect us from the elements. It keeps us warm in the winter, provides a barrier between us and sun and wind, and keeps dirt away from our skin. It is meant to work with the body and environment, not against it.

Yet consider the results of a recent Greenpeace report on dangerous chemicals in household products. Among those items tested were children's pyjamas – the kind emblazoned with colourful plastic transfers of popular cartoon characters that can be found wrapped around little bodies throughout the UK for eight or more hours a day.

In this survey, widely available branded pyjamas emblazoned with pictures of friendly cartoon characters were amongst the most polluted items surveyed, containing high levels of nonylphenol, which can interfere with human DNA and affect sperm production in mammals, and phthalates, which can cause liver, kidney and testicular damage. These harmful, hormone-disrupting chemicals, the report said, were probably in the garments as a result of the inks and PVC plastic film used in the design on the front.

The textile industry is one of the most polluting in the world, using thousands of chemicals known to be dangerous to human health and wildlife in the manufacture of material for clothing and furnishing. The overuse of pesticides on textile crops has led to pesticide resistance, causing farmers to spray more chemicals with less and less effect. Today, approximately 8,000 chemicals are routinely used in the production, processing and treatment of conventional textiles.

LIFTING THE LID

Statistics reveal the cotton used in one standard, conventional T-shirt requires 140g (5oz) of synthetic pesticides and fertilisers to grow – equivalent to a cup of sugar.

One of the most common reactions to conventionally produced textiles is contact dermatitis. It has also been shown that the frequency of textile-dye allergy is increasing with up to 16 per cent of people reacting to something in the clothes they wear. Any one of several things, including rubber materials, chemical additives, glues and tanning agents are known irritants. Occasionally, the formaldehyde finishing resins used to make cotton or cotton/polyester-blend fabrics wrinkle-resistant are implicated in skin irritation. So are the flame retardants Tris (2,3-dibromopropyl) phosphate and 2,3- dibromocresylglycidyl ether.

But often it is the dyes used on our textiles that cause the allergic reactions. The nature of the fabric determines what type of dye is used. Most reported allergic reactions have been to what are known as 'dispersal dyes'. These dyes are loosely held on the fabric structure and easily rubbed off on the skin. These types of dyes are commonly used on synthetic fabrics. For contact dermatitis sufferers, dyes such as disperse blue dyes 106 and 124, and some yellows, reds and oranges are most commonly implicated.

Some chemicals routinely found in textiles are associated with longer-term health risks. A recent Swedish study showed that the hazardous chemicals that can most commonly be detected on clothes are the result of biocides (pesticides, fungicides, etc.), flame retardants, azo and dispersion dyes, carriers (adjuvants for polyester/wool-mixture dyeing), fabric softeners and formaldehydes.

Research from the Danish Environmental Protection Agency confirms this. A chemical analysis of everyday textiles revealed the presence of, among other things, naphthalene, o-chlorophenol, nicotine, several phthalates, quaternary ammonium compounds, nonylphenol ethoxylates, a range of benzenes, toluenes and amines and polycyclic compounds as well as the heavy metals lead, cadmium, copper, cobalt, chromium, nickel, zinc, barium, tin, arsenic and mercury. This list of chemicals includes known carcinogens as well as reproductive and nervous system toxins.

Phthalates are another common clothing additive. These plasticising chemicals are oestrogenic and potentially carcinogenic. They are currently banned from teething toys for the under 3s but are widely used in the plastics that decorate children's clothes. Children who chew and suck on bits of their clothing may end up ingesting these compounds, which build up in the body over time.

Similarly, apart from their potential for triggering allergy, azo dyes are carcinogenic and both the German and Danish governments have now outlawed many of these, though their use elsewhere in the world continues to be widespread. Some Chinese factories have now stopped using them as a result of the pressure from Germany.

Environmental impacts

The longer-term risks of conventional textiles also extend to the environment. The various stages of textile production (from spinning, weaving and knitting to dyeing and finishing) also require enormous amounts of energy and water; for example, 100 litres of water are needed to process one kilogram of textiles. Around 70 per cent of textile effluents and 20 per cent of dyestuffs are dumped into water supplies by clothing factories. In addition, clothing, footwear and accessories are a staple of municipal landfills. The wider environment can be affected when water becomes polluted during their manufacture.

Cotton, the world's favourite textile, is useful for a huge range of purposes from underpants to soft furnishings. After tobacco, cotton is the second most pesticide-dependent crop in the world, accounting for 10 per cent of global pesticide use and 25 per cent of insecticides. It is also a thirsty crop requiring vast amounts of water to grow.

In some cotton-farming areas, five of the nine most common pesticides used on cotton are known carcinogens. Similarly, wool – another commonly used material for bedding – is subject to many chemical treatments while it is on the sheep's back, including neurotoxic organophosphate dips which have been linked to debilitating illness among sheep farmers. Traces of these pesticides can remain in the finished cloth.

Going natural

One in three UK consumers are making lifestyle choices and are purchasing eco-friendly products, and the UK organic food market has expanded massively and is currently worth around £920 million per year. But the concept of making and buying organic textiles – though increasing in popularity – has not yet reached the stage of a revolution, or even a movement.

Nevertheless, natural textiles – whether they are organic or not – have several advantages over synthetics. They allow the skin to breathe and are generally hard-wearing and adaptable. When such fabrics are organically produced, their advantages multiply for both the wearer and the environment.

The range of organic options for children is growing all the time. While once upon a time organic clothes might have been a style-free collection of shapeless, 'practical' garments in muted colours of off-

NATURALLY COLOURED COTTON

Materials that are suspected, or proven, to cause other illnesses or conditions such as cancer or allergies are not allowed in UK organic textiles. Unfortunately, nearly all commercial textiles, including the textiles identified as 'low-impact' and 'organic', allow the use of synthetic petrochemical dyes because truly organic alternatives are rare and not available in high volumes. In this respect organic does not always equate with botanical.

Safe dyes appear to be one of the fashion industry's biggest hurdles. Some producers of organic cottons, however, are working on developing very unique cotton strains through traditional hybridisation techniques (see Fox Fibre in the Resources section). Organic cotton can be grown naturally in shades of natural greens, beiges and browns as well as ivory. Naturally coloured cotton is not new or unique. The Inca used it, as did ancient Egyptian and Indian cultures as well as the Native Americans. When you can find it, this is undoubtedly the most eco-friendly option.

TRY THIS INSTEAD

Natural and organic clothing is still a little more expensive than non-organic and is most commonly available via mail order. However, there are many compelling health and environmental reasons to consider when weighing it up against its more readily available and often cheaper conventional counterparts.

- **Dress your baby in organic fibres where possible**. Nappies are the obvious place to start (see Chapter 4) but t-shirts, vests and sleepsuits – really anything which is likely to be next to your baby's skin for long periods of time – can be made that much safer by switching to organic. Popular choices include cotton, wool, silk and more recently, hemp.
- **Look carefully at labels.** Many companies and even environmental organizations offer clothes, bedding and tote bags made from unbleached, conventionally grown cotton. The off-white appearance of the fabric, and the claim of 'natural' can make consumers believe they are buying a truly ecological item. Unbleached cotton is only a half solution. It may not contain chlorides but can still contain harmful pesticides.
- **Reuse.** Instead of buying new clothes for your baby, consider second-hand. Firstly, it is environmentally friendly. Secondly, chemical residues diminish somewhat with washing so second-hand baby clothes will contain less of these. Babies don't need to fashionable; they need to be comfortable and safe. Many mother-and-baby groups have clothing swaps that can save money and are eco-friendly since they divert clothes from landfill.
- The Resources section can help you find companies that can supply good quality clothing for your child and for the whole family. When you are finished with the clothes, repeat the cycle by giving them away rather than disposing to landfill.

white and beige, organic clothing has started to make more of a fashion statement in recent years.

In the UK, the Soil Association helped move things along by producing its own standards for organic textiles including wool, hemp, linen, cotton, skins and leather products. This means that consumers may well start seeing the Soil Association logo on clothes and other materials, which will help you to make informed choices about the ecological impact of the clothes you're buying.

For a garment to be labelled organic by the Soil Association, its raw materials must contain at least 95 per cent organic materials, excluding accessories such as buttons and zips. If an item contains 70–94 per cent organic materials it must be labelled 'made with XX per cent organic materials'

This means that the use of herbicides is prohibited and synthetic pesticides are severely restricted. All animals will be reared to organic standards and no genetically modified (GM) inputs are allowed.

Natural dyes from plants or insects that have been organically produced must be used where available in sufficient quality and quantity. The Soil Association also says that petrochemical-derived plastic should not be used where an alternative exists, and justification must be provided for the use of some non-organic fibres in products which cannot be made without their inclusion, like socks and tights.

A lick of paint

Lots of parents spend a fortune decorating a new nursery only to find that their baby ends up sleeping with them often for the first few months or longer. From the paint on the walls to the bed your baby sleeps in, there are good reasons to not go overboard preparing a special nursery.

A fresh coat of paint, for instance, is a quick, cost-effective way to give even the scruffiest space a new lease on life. Yet we seldom stop to consider the ingredients that make up the average tin of interior paint. Not that long ago, interior and exterior paints contained the heavy metals lead and mercury. Although this is no longer the case, many cases of sick-building syndrome have been traced to other substances in interior paints, which include solvents and other volatile organic compounds (VOCs).

Household paint is made from a complex mixture of chemicals with functions not dissimilar to many cosmetics. They contain carrier oils, dispersion agents, viscosity adjusters, thickeners, surface tension adjusters, plasticisers and preservatives, and most contain synthetic colours. Some contain antifungal agents such as arsenic disulfide, phenol, formaldehyde and quaternary ammonium compounds.

Modern emulsions are water-based, with vinyl or acrylic resins added to make them more hard-wearing. The amount of resin determines the varying degrees of sheen seen in matt, eggshell, silk and satin finishes. Gloss paints are oil-based and include resins to give them a hard-wearing quality.

The 'clean' smell of new paint is actually vapour released from these chemicals as the paint dries. This off-gassing can carry on for days, months and in some cases years after the paint has been applied.

Common VOCs in paints, primers and varnishes include benzene, formaldehyde, kerosene, ammonia, toluene and xylene, all of which are known carcinogens and neurotoxins. Exposure to VOCs can irritate your eyes, nose, throat and skin and are proven to increase allergies, asthma and respiratory problems, central nervous system symptoms (such as headache, rapid heartbeat) and even weaken the immune system. They can also be harmful to the liver and kidneys. To further complicate the issue, it is now known that it is possible for two or more 'less harmful' VOCs to combine to create a more powerful toxin.

LIFTING THE LID

The US Environmental Protection Agency (EPA) ranks paint on its top-five list of environmental hazards. A study conducted by the agency found that VOC levels indoors can be a thousand times higher than outdoor levels when an indoor paint is drying. Another study found that the application and drying of paint releases VOCs at a higher rate than any other product used indoors.

Research published in 2005 showed that exposure to VOCs increases the risk of childhood asthma, something that should give parents painting children's rooms pause for thought.

The chemicals used in ordinary paint production are bad for the wider environment as well. For every tonne of paint produced, the resulting waste can be anything up to 30 tonnes. This waste doesn't degrade naturally and once in the soil or air can be persistent and toxic.

Safer alternatives exist. Some paints contain no chemical solvents, while other more widely available commercial brands just contain a lower percentage of VOCs than conventional paints. Eco-friendly paints make use of ingredients such as turpentine or d-limonene as alternatives to white spirit. Instead of plastic binders they may use linseed oil or casein, and chalk and clay may replace fillers such as titanium dioxide. Colours are often derived from natural earth and mineral pigments. See the Resources section for companies that produce safe, natural paints for your home.

Better bedding

The habit of isolating babies in a room by themselves to sleep is a relatively new one in human history. For most of our evolution, family groups slept together for protection, for comfort and for warmth.

Before you spend a lot of money on a cot or crib, consider your options. Co-sleeping, for instance, is a safe and comforting way of settling in with a new baby, it makes night-time breastfeeding much easier and causes less disruption to parents' sleep since they don't have to get up to comfort a crying baby. If a baby sleeps in his parents' bed he is less likely to wake frequently in the night and is more likely to settle quickly if he does wake.

Even if you are not happy with the idea of your baby sleeping in the

LIFTING THE LID

In two recent studies comparing conventional and organic crib mattresses, organic cotton mattresses were the only ones studied that don't give off toxic fumes.

same bed as you, the evidence suggests that a baby who sleeps in a simple cot in his parents' room is at reduced risk of sudden infant death syndrome (SIDS).

A good night's sleep is important for babies and parents since sleep is the time that the body does its 'housekeeping' by resetting, repairing and reordering all its working systems for the following day ahead. Adequate sleep is also important in boosting immunity and regulating blood sugar.

> *Flame retardants build up in the body and have been linked to learning and behavioural problems in children*

While a good option for a first bed is a traditional Moses basket – made from natural wicker or grass – that sits on a sturdy stand, most babies will quickly outgrow these (another reason for considering co-sleeping). Make sure the mattress in the basket is made of natural materials like latex or coir (made from coconut shells) or stuffed with wool.

NATURAL FLEECES

One hundred per cent lambskin fleeces are excellent for giving sleeping babies a sense of comfort and security no matter where they are. Fleeces are lightweight, so they can be carried anywhere and used on the floor, or in a cot, crib or Moses basket. The benefits of lambskin fleeces include:

- They are sanitary: lambskin fleeces are both bactericidal and dirt-repellent (viruses and bacteria can't breed in protein, and lambskins are 100 per cent protein)
- They insulate against both heat and cold: they keep babies warm in winter and cool in summer
- They're naturally fire retardant
- They're breathable: a baby sleeping on his front can breathe through the fibres

TRY THIS INSTEAD

The choice is entirely yours, of course, but if you are concerned that chemicals in your bedding may be adding significantly to your child's total toxic load then you need to ask yourself if you can afford to *not* go natural or organic. Consider these other options for a healthy environment for your baby's bedroom:

- **Buy second-hand.** Every day in the UK around 3,000 tonnes of reusable wood is sent to landfill or burned. Buying second-hand or borrowing prolongs the useful life of furniture and is more eco-friendly since it does not use up new resources. If you are worried about using a second-hand mattress you can always put a new, natural mattress in an old crib.
- **Avoid fake wood** such as nursery furniture made from composite materials like MDF. This is made by gluing together thin layers of wood with strong glue and can give off harmful gases like formaldehyde and other volatile chemicals.
- **Buy solid wooden furniture** in preference to plastic. Look for the FSC logo on new nursery furniture that guarantees the wood is traceable back to a sustainably managed forest. Consider also buying furniture made from reclaimed wood or new green materials like bamboo or coconut.
- **Use organic textiles** for curtains, cushions, crib bumpers and rugs. Look for cotton sheets and pillowcases made from untreated natural organic fibres; perhaps your parents or grandparents have got some in the attic?
- **Buy a mattress made from natural materials.** This can be a latex base or one that is stuffed with wool or hemp fibres, covered with organic cotton. Natural fibres are also breathable and allow sweat to evaporate, so cooling your baby down. If using a second-hand or conventional mattress, consider an organic cotton mattress pad. Look for the Soil Association logo on natural and organic mattresses. These will meet all fire-safety standards without having been treated with harmful chemicals.

Ctd

- **If you use a regular mattress,** cover it with several layers of old cotton blankets washed in a non-scented soap or just plain baking soda.
- **Learn to sew.** If you or a kindly relative can sew, make a casing for the crib bumpers out of a heavy barrier cotton cloth that keeps the toxic plasticisers and formaldehyde stuffing fumes to a minimum. Or, start from scratch by making a crib bumper from cotton cloth, stuffed with organic cotton.
- **Wood flooring** is the best flooring since it does not collect dust and other allergens and does not give off harmful gases like synthetic carpets.

Polyurethane foam mattresses break down and release chemicals that are known carcinogens. Both mattress and bedding are usually sprayed with chemical fire retardants which have been linked with respiratory problems and skin allergies.

Conventional carry-cots tend to be made of plastic which can give off toxic fumes. Conventional cot mattresses tend to be made from polyurethane foam and PVC, both of which are energy intensive to make, don't biodegrade and can give off toxic fumes. Chlorinated phosphate compounds – which are cancer-causing – and melamine (the same stuff used to coat wooden floors), are routinely used to treat most polyurethane foam mattresses to make them flame retardant. Phosphorus is also reportedly still used as a fire retardant in conventional cotton mattresses. The most recent evidence suggests that the off-gassing from infant bedding is an important, but often overlooked, cause of cot-death. Flame retardants also build up in the body over time and have been linked to learning and behavioural problems in children.

In 1977 the flame retardant TRIS (2,3 dibomopropyl) phosphate, a known carcinogen, was finally banned for use in children's sleepwear. At the time of the ban it was estimated that 50 to 60 million children wore TRIS-treated garments. TRIS has been shown to affect kidney, liver and lung function and to cause mutations in some bacteria. In animals it has caused testicular shrinkage and reduced the reproductive capacity of females. Although banned in clothing, TRIS remains a danger to children because it is still used as a flame retardant in polyurethane foam, car-seat cushions and other consumer products.

Non-toxic toys

No one would deny the importance of play in a child's life. From the earliest age, play is the way children explore, learn and make sense of their world. Yet no subject is charged with more confusion or debate than play things. On the one hand, parents may throw their hands up in horror at both the price and the appropriateness of the latest electronic gadget, but on the other, wooden toys, or those toys that run on brain cells instead of battery cells, can sometimes require more substantial parental input in the play session.

Television has changed the way that families engage with one another, replacing interaction with passive gratification. More and more, electronic and computer games are made so that children can play on their own. Because we have become so accustomed to the idea that toys are something to keep children busy and quiet, we seem to have forgotten that toys are one of the primary ways in which our children learn and that learning is more enjoyable when parents are involved.

As your children get older, board games can be a great way of introducing basic maths to them, construction toys fuel a child's curiosity about how things work; while fantasy play provides a way of exploring the wide world in the safety of a child's own home, as well as a welcome break from more 'institutionalised' forms of play allowed during school time.

This debate is complicated enough, but recent recalls of so-called dangerous toys have raised parents' awareness not only of what toys are for, but what they are made of.

In August 2007, Mattel, the world's largest toy maker, recalled 18 million toys worldwide and two million toys in the UK, saying they posed a safety risk. The targets of the recall included Polly Pocket, Barbie and Batman (over fears that magnets could come loose and be swallowed by young children) and 49,000 Chinese-made toy cars, (over fears they contained excessive levels of lead in the paint). Just a week before the recall, Fisher Price, owned by Mattel, pulled nearly 100,000 toys off UK shelves, over similar fears that they were covered with poisonous paint.

Other manufacturers may not be as diligent in protecting the public – or their workers. Around 75 per cent of the world's toys are manufactured in China, where there are nearly 10,000 toy factories. This means that the average child's toy sold in the US or Europe is likely to have been made in a crowded sweatshop by a Chinese peasant girl paid pittance wages, wearing no protective clothing and enjoying little in the way of worker rights. Contrast that with the average toy executive on a big salary, overseeing million-pound marketing budgets, and you will get some idea of what the world's toy market has become. Today, children the world over play with the same plastic action figures, dolls and film tie-in characters which, it could be argued, teach them more about brand loyalty and the value of conforming than anything else.

Most toys are made from petroleum-based plastic, and even some seemingly benign wooden ones are subjected to a number of harmful toxic processes and ingredients before they reach the shelves. So the next time you buy a toy for your or someone else's child think not just about the gift, but the kind of world you are buying into.

Think also about the hidden health implications of what you are buying. For instance, Canadian research concluded that children weighing less than 8.2kg (18lb) who suck on products such as teethers and rattles made with di-isononyl phthalate (DINP) for more than three hours a day run the risk of liver enlargement or kidney scarring.

RETHINK STORAGE

Brightly coloured plastics in a child's room, such as storage crates, may look modern and clean, but they continually give off toxic formaldehyde gas that is implicated in respiratory problems and has also been shown to be carcinogenic. Formaldehyde also comes from soft furnishings, vinyl wallpapers, insulation, varnishes, new carpets, upholstery and new mattresses. We may not always be able to smell these gases but they are continually entering our bodies and have the potential to cause harm. When considering storage units for toys, untreated wood boxes, traditional wooden toy chests and baskets made from natural grasses are a healthier alternative.

The European Commission agrees that soft PVC toys are potentially very dangerous. The Commission points to scientific evidence that shows that those made from PVC, and thus a softening chemical called phthalates, can pose a serious health threat, possible causing liver, kidney and testicular damage, which is why toys and teethers made from soft PVC material are now banned for under-3s.

Children's toys can contain other hazards as well. Lead and cadmium are used in the manufacture of soft chewy toys, to help stabilise the vinyl. Ingestion of these can result in brain and nervous system damage (in the case of lead) and cancer and kidney disease (in the case of cadmium). Recently in the US, a major health scare came about when it was discovered that crayons contained asbestos. Crayon manufacturers use talc to coat the finished product and talc is frequently contaminated with asbestos.

There has also been concern expressed in the medical press that the current trend for noisy toys – the ones which squeak, squawk and sing, may be damaging our children's hearing. According to the report, squeaky, brightly coloured toys for babies and toy motor vehicles may

THE STERILISING QUESTION

Sterilising baby bottles, toys and clothes is completely unnecessary. The germs in your home are those which you and your family are used to. They are unlikely to produce anything which your baby cannot cope with, particularly if you are breastfeeding and thus passing on some of your own immunity.

In contrast, traces of disinfectant on clothes, bottles and toys can be harmful to baby's delicate skin and if ingested could make the baby sick.

Take the hint from our hospitals, which are supposed to pay closer attention to the process of killing germs than most other environments. Not only do they find it impossible to be completely sterile, but their efforts have contributed to the growth of 'superbugs', those bacteria immune to the strongest bleaches, the most powerful antibacterial cleaners and to antibiotic medicines.

emit sounds of 78 to 108 decibels (dB). When held at arm's length, such toys may reach 112 dB. At a child's ear toy mobile phones may emit 122 dB and toy weapons may emit as much as 150 to 160 dB – well over what it would take to cause damage children's delicate ears.

TRY THIS INSTEAD

An estimated 13 million toys end up in landfill sites each year, so before you buy, think about the whole life-cycle of a toy. The toys you buy your children should be safe for them, and cause no harm to the planet or to the people who made them. Several companies now produce ethical and engaging toys and these are detailed in the Resources section of this book. Consider also this new-toy checklist:

- **Non-toxic** Children will put anything in their mouths, so don't buy toys made from PVC plastic, which may include phthalates, the suspected hormone-disruptors that have also been linked to liver and kidney damage. Instead, choose toys made from natural materials such as wood, hemp and cotton. Wooden toys should not be made using toxic azo dyes, leaded paints or chemical preservatives such as formaldehyde. Choose toys that use non-toxic dyes and natural oil finishes such as linseed, walnut oil and beeswax, all of which are safe.
- **Sweatshop-free** Choosing toys that have been made with high ethical standards, such as those of the Fairtrade Foundation, will ensure that workers get fair wages for their work and that there has been no abuse of child labour.
- **Natural materials** like wood are ideal, but be aware. Wooden toys should not be made from old-growth forest destruction. Look for toys certified by the Forest Stewardship Council, or an equivalent guarantor of responsible forestry, to ensure that old-growth and endangered trees are preserved.
- **No unnecessary packaging** Many children's toys are packaged inside oversized boxes and wrapped in layer upon layer of plastic wrap. This is completely unnecessary for the product.

Toys should not replace parental attention, they should augment it, particularly when children are young. And while they may not be specifically organic, they can be made healthier for the mind – and if they are made with non-toxic ingredients, for the body too. When choosing toys for your baby, consider those that are made from sustainable wood and recycled, unbleached untreated, chemical-free or organic fabrics. Electronic toys are not suitable for younger children.

Getting around

When you are pregnant, carrying your baby around is easy. Wherever you go, the baby goes too. But what happens when you want the same degree of mobility after the baby is born?

When your baby is very small, a sling is the safest, most secure and most comfortable place for him or her to be. Snuggled next to mum's chest your baby is warm, secure and if you are breastfeeding, close to food. Carrying a baby in a sling is almost a forgotten art. Widely practised in non-industrialised countries, the Western world seems to have shed the sling in favour of the pram. Slings, however, offer emotional and physical benefits to both baby and parents.

Baby slings have many benefits:

Emotional
- Babies in slings can hear their parent's heartbeat and voice and smell their scent, helping to make them feel emotionally secure.
- Babies are naturally rocked as their parents move about: babies in slings are easily comforted and tend to cry less.
- Slings allow parents to respond instantly to their babies' needs.
- It's easier for mothers to breastfeed babies in slings.

Physical
- Slings help babies maintain constant body temperature.
- They take away the strain of carrying your baby: slings offer back and hip support.
- Babies in slings are above the level of car exhaust emissions, which hang around at the same height as most prams.

Convenience
- In urban areas, slings are much more convenient than prams for navigating the doors, stairs and tight spaces of public transport.
- Hands-free slings, in contrast to holding babies using one arm and their hip, allow parents the use of both arms. No need to open packets with one hand and your teeth, or to develop bulging muscles in your regular carrying arm.

There are two main types of sling:

- **Vertical or hands-free slings** carry a newborn baby in the frog position by supporting their thighs, hips and pelvis. Look for those that give support to the baby's head and neck. Babies over 6 months old can face outwards and observe the world around them at eye level: a perfect height for babies to be smiled at by others, unlike in a pram.
- **Horizontal or side slings** are hammock-style slings that allow babies to lie down while being carried, but parents will need to support newborns with one hand. They support babies from birth in a natural cradling position in front, which places no strain on newborn babies' immature back muscles.

As your baby grows, the pushchair becomes the vehicle of choice. Over the last few decades, pushchairs and prams have gone through some major design changes. What were once cumbersome machines designed for brief forays into the fresh air have become the infant equivalent of the four-wheel drive. Some have even been developed in conjunction with all-terrain vehicle manufacturers!

Parents are demanding lighter vehicles with better all-round support for the babies, and manufacturers are keen to meet the demand. The result has been a proliferation of all-terrain pushchairs that are easier to steer (as in the three-wheel variety) and more and more design features to improve their durability as well as their comfort for baby, their convenience for mums and their 'street cred' for dads.

Even if your child is lying flat – essential for newborns – all-terrain buggies are not really suitable for babies under 3 months. It is simply not good for little babies to be jiggled around over rocks and across ploughed fields. However, once your child is older you might appreciate the greater mobility which these vehicles have to offer.

When choosing a pushchair remember:

- **Be sensible**. Go for a lightweight and durable model instead of an over-designed variety. Your baby doesn't need a cup holder, he or she needs good support and materials that are, as far as possible, non toxic.
- **Aim high**. For many babies, an afternoon out in the low-slung pushchair is a toxic trip. Look for a pushchair that sits your baby higher than exhaust-pipe level.
- **Borrow, or buy second-hand**. Most pushchairs are made from energy-intensive materials and are used only for short periods of time before being given — or worse — tossed away when they still have plenty of useful life left in them.
- **Avoid travel systems** that turn from car seats to carry-cots to pushchairs. Studies show that parents tend to leave their babies strapped in these for longer than is healthy. Apart from the fact that these are usually made of heavy plastic and man-made fibres, the angle babies sit at can put a strain on their bodies. A baby's head can become flattened at the back from being against a hard-backed carry-cot for long periods of time.

Chapter 6

Simplify Your Life

Most parents know that the greatest gift they can give their children is good health. Once upon a time this may have seemed like a simple matter of putting a roof over their heads, making sure they had a good winter coat and giving them decent food. The rest, parents may have reasoned, was up to chance, genetics or Divine intervention.

Today, life is more complex. We live in a polluted world surrounded daily by hundreds of man-made toxins that we can't see, taste or even smell but which nevertheless have the potential to damage human health. When we go to the supermarket we buy 'fresh' foods which are covered with pesticides and not really fresh at all. Instead they are stored for long periods of time during which they are sprayed with even more chemicals to maintain the appearance of freshness. As our schedules get busier we rely more and more on convenience foods laced with additives, flavourings, colours and aromas, all of which can cause a variety of health problems.

The idea of 'natural parenting' has become a buzzword in the media lately – a hook to write articles around and a platform from which to sell a variety of new products. In a society where everything is geared towards giving us a hassle-free lifestyle, where quality is often compromised for convenience, it is easy to caricature so-called natural parents until they seem ridiculous enough to scorn. These are, we tell ourselves, the parents indulging in a new kind of consumer counter-culture. They dress their children in 100 per cent organic cotton, use nutrition, herbs and homeopathy to deal with illness, sleep with their babies on 100 per cent cotton futon-type mattresses. They breastfeed until the child is well into its third year, supplementing this with only organic home-made baby food and snacks made from largely unprocessed ingredients. The natural parent buys only wooden toys, knitted dolls and beeswax crayons to use on recycled paper.

In reality 'natural parents' come in all shapes and sizes and with all sorts of reasons for wanting to give their children a more natural start in life. There is no such thing as a perfect green parent; we all make some compromises. But as our world gets increasingly complex, and information on the effects of environmental pollution becomes more readily available to the general public, many parents want to make the world inside and outside the home cleaner and healthier for their children. If you believe the hype, the best way to do this is to buy the green alternatives for everything. But even this is problematical. Remember that sometimes the greenest alternative is not to buy at all.

Parents spend an average of £10,000 in the first few years of their baby's life. We're buying more for babies than ever before. But do we really need all this paraphernalia?

If you believe that buying lots of stuff for your baby is an external sign of how much you love her, or that the need to buy lots of baby stuff is just 'the way things are' then you have been duped into worshipping at the altar of consumer society where the accumulation of 'things' is the only worthy goal. Step back for a moment and allow yourself to believe that the thing your child needs most is you.

It's all too easy to point the finger of blame at advertisers for misleading and influencing us. The power of advertising – in its overt form such as billboards and TV ads, but also in its subtle form such as the editorial content of many parenting and women's magazines – is strong. It plays on our fears, worries and dissatisfaction with ourselves. In particular, it plays on parents' fears that they may not have the inner resources to cope with raising a child, so the stuff we can buy is then offered up as a resource substitute.

But as consumers we are also part of the problem. Our thoughtless demands for more throwaway stuff – plastic containers, wrinkle-free and stain-resistant fabrics, wash-and-go toiletries and household cleaners and ready made everything – decimate the planet and add to the problem of pollution. If we stopped buying unnecessary 'stuff', there would be no reason for manufacturers to produce it, and without the demand this convenience culture of ours would die away.

Truly natural parenting is much more than substituting one manufacturer's 'stuff' for another's. At heart it is about building information and support networks, and building confidence so that parents feel able to follow their instincts about raising and protecting their children. It encompasses a concern for the environment in which our children will grow and prosper, with a longer-term eye on things that can affect our children's health and development.

As parents we have it in our power to think and do things differently. We can rethink what we buy and why we buy it. We can begin to change the way we live and parent in order to reduce our impact on the planet and our exposure to toxic chemicals. We can demand that manufacturers stop putting toxins in everyday products. We can make an investment in our community, for goods and services, and if we find the local area is lacking, take action to demand that better local services are put there to support us.

You have the power to change things. If you are ready to apply the brakes on parenting as a consumer sport, and on a toxic modern lifestyle that is accelerating out of control, consider these first simple steps:

Buy less

We buy and eat too much food. We buy and often only half-use too many toiletries and cosmetics. We buy too much stuff for babies in the belief that the investment in wipes, mega packs of nappies, brand labels and plastic toys makes us good parents. Get off the treadmill. Ignore all those '3-for-2' offers that supermarkets use to offload products they have too many of. Think about what you really need, what is essential to your life, and to the wellbeing of your baby, and stick to it.

Reuse, repair, recycle

Some time after Word War II, the concepts of doing without, making do and sticking to the necessities became practically unpatriotic, and somewhere along the way the personal freedom fought for got confused with the freedom to buy things, to have things, to show off to others the things you have and be envied for them. As a result, many of the skills that sustained our forefathers have fallen out of fashion. It's not just that we don't know how to build our own barns or grow our own food. Many of us don't know how to knit a blanket, repair clothing or make a meal from scratch. Frugality too has gone out of fashion, but in a world rapidly running out of resources it's time to resurrect that as well.

Keep local

Once you have a baby, your community and neighbourhood become important sources of support. It can be hard to shop if you have no local retailers or a car – but remember, supermarkets and superstores are the reason for this and the way most of us shop today has fostered the demise of the local shopkeeper. The more we support them, the more they will proliferate. There are plenty of online stores from which you can now order quality products – everything from nappies to toys and clothes and even baby food. Now's the time to ask yourself, 'How well do I know my local area?', 'Are there people who offer goods and services that I can and should be taking advantage of?' If so, then do it.

Don't be dazzled by brands

Particularly when you are buying food or toiletries, brand loyalty may mean that you are getting poor value for money and may be exposing yourself to more chemicals than you have to. By learning to read the label and compare products you will find that there is often little difference between brands, that cheaper brands are just as good and that there are low chemical options for almost everything you buy. Likewise, buying second-hand can be a good antidote to brand slavery. As well as being cheaper and more frugal with the earth's resources, it is a good way to step off the brand-name treadmill every once in a while.

Embrace simplicity

Many of the pollutants and toxins we encounter every day are the result of our unbridled consumerism, so choose not to buy into this unhealthy addiction. The fact is, the less stuff you have in your life, the less likely you are to come in contact with environmental toxins.

If you only use the microwave to heat up coffee or bake potatoes, perhaps the time has come to get rid of this significant source of radiation in your home altogether. If you de-clutter your home, chances are you will not need so many plastic boxes to store things – reducing these means less formaldehyde gas in the air. Likewise, if you use fewer cosmetics, toiletries, air fresheners and harsh household cleaners, you will be reducing your exposure, and your baby's exposure, to solvents and other VOCs as well as environmental hormone mimics.

Cultivating simplicity in your life is not just some vague hippie dream. These days, it requires an iron will to resist advertising pressure to buy more stuff and consume more than you need. Dig deep and see if you can find that will!

Parenthood as a spiritual journey

No matter how hard we try to simplify parenting on the outside, on the inside it can be a challenging job and one that changes us, and changes the things we believe, forever.

The Ancient Chinese believed that pregnancy was a spiritual practice which lasted for nine months. During this time the mother was expected to spend her time in quiet contemplation and prayer. She would surround herself with pleasant things – mental, emotional and spiritual. This gave her inner strength and a solid ground to stand on. And since the mother's physical and spiritual wellbeing has a direct influence on the foetus, it also provided the baby with a strong foundation.

Looked at from the perspective of our culture, this view of pregnancy may seem quaint. Yet we know that a baby in the womb responds to its mother's emotions. For instance, studies have shown that babies move less and even grow less well when their mothers are anxious. Some psychotherapists believe that the experience – good and bad – of being inside of our mothers remains with us for life.

Not every pregnant women welcomes such information though. Perhaps this is because nearly every pregnant woman has had a moment when she wished she was not pregnant, or that life could go back to the way it was before the coloured line on the home pregnancy test changed her life so completely.

Some, however, don't feel threatened by the idea that the baby can 'read' their thoughts. Instead, they believe, as some therapists do, that the baby can benefit from experiencing its mother's full range of emotions; that such an experience forms the basis of the child's emotional education.

Of course, it's not just the child whose life is profoundly affected by the time spent inside its mother. For many women, carrying a child, being aware of the pulse of a new life pounding within them, is the catalyst for re-evaluating the way they live, who they are and their place in the world. It becomes a time to review priorities and decide the extent to which they will allow the conventions and values of the world at large to influence their personal behaviour.

Your philosophy of life

Apart from acquiring practical skills and a bit more consumer savvy, some prospective parents become acutely aware of the need for a kind of spiritual re-education which includes a review of their priorities and their philosophy of life.

Pregnancy throws up certain questions about life as we experience it. For instance: 'What's important to me in this life?', 'What are my principles?', 'What do I care about?', 'What am I willing to stand up for and what am I not willing to stand up for?' 'What do I want to pass on?' These are the questions which form the basis of your individual life philosophy. Such questions also provide the basis for all the choices women make about themselves, their babies and their care during pregnancy.

Perhaps you've never done this sort of personal inventory before. It may seem daunting to even contemplate it. But if you are up to it, the most useful way to begin is to get a sheet of paper (or two) and just write out your 'philosophy' about life. Typically this would include some statement as to why you think we're here on Earth, what it is that you believe we are supposed to do while we are here, what you think is important in life (and what is not important), and which values of our society you agree with and which you do not.

For those who wish to take the exercise further, below are some of the other elements which go into making an individual life philosophy. You can use any of these (though you don't have to use all of them) or you may simply choose to write out what you feel inside yourself. Either way, don't expect the answers to come easily or necessarily even

116

to make sense immediately. Some answers may seem simple and straightforward to you, others may not. You may want to contemplate the issues raised over a longer period of time. Having begun to think of these things, don't be surprised if any problems that you are currently experiencing begin to take on a new dimension – either they become more complex or suddenly simpler than you thought.

- **Beauty** What is beautiful to you? How important is it in your life?
- **Behaviour** How do you think we should behave in this world?
- **Beliefs** What are your strongest beliefs?
- **Choice** What do you think about its nature and importance?
- **Community** In what ways do we belong to each other and what do you think our responsibility is to each other?
- **Compassion** Why do you think it's important and what are the best/most appropriate ways to express it in our daily life?
- **Confusion or ambivalence** Is it a normal part of life? How much do you think we need to learn to live with it?
- **Death** What do you think about it and what do you think happens after it?
- **Events** What do you think makes things happen and how do we explain this to ourselves?
- **Evil** Is there such a thing? How do you identify/define it?
- **Free will** Are things pre-ordained to happen or do we have free will?
- **God/Supreme Being** Do you have a concept of One? If so, what do you think the Supreme Being is like? What does the Supreme Being mean in and demand of your life?
- **Heroes/Heroines** Who are yours? Why?
- **Human** What do you think makes somebody truly human?
- **Individuality** In what ways do we stand alone? What does it mean to be an individual?
- **Love** What do you think is its nature and importance? What qualities do you relate to love (e.g., grace, forgiveness, trust, etc.)?
- **Morality** What is it? Which issues concern you most?
- **Principles** Which ones are you willing to stand up for and which ones do you base your life on?
- **Purpose** Why do you think we are here on this earth? What would you say is the purpose of your life?

- **Reality** What can you say about the nature of reality?
- **Sacrifice** What in life is worth sacrificing for and what would you be willing to sacrifice?
- **Self** What do you believe about yourself, your ego, selfishness and selflessness?
- **Stewardship** What do you think we should do with God's gifts to us?
- **Truth** What is the truth and in what areas is it most important to you?
- **Values** What are the ones you hold most dear, sacred and important?
- **Violence** What is violence? Is it a physical, mental and/or emotional phenomenon? Is it ever justified?

Looking over such a list you may still be wondering, what's all this got to do with being pregnant? Yet, when you are carrying another life inside of you, issues like stewardship, love, faith, ambivalence, sacrifice, death, individuality and free will are with you every day. They are with you when you decide about antenatal tests, when you think ahead to labour, when you experience ups and downs with your partner and in the middle of the night when you wonder 'Who am I?' and 'What resources do I have to cope with parenthood?'

One of the reasons why the subjects on this list seem so daunting is because we rarely take the time to think about what they mean to us or to look for the places where they influence our lives. If you've never done such an exercise before it can be quite an eye opener. Often people find, for example, that although they thought they had strong principles they can suddenly think of rather too many times when they have compromised these. Or it dawns on them that they have never really given death and dying much consideration or that their views about death have changed dramatically since becoming pregnant.

Your individual life philosophy isn't just for your benefit, though. The fact is that conception, not birth, is the beginning of parenthood. While it is common to feel that as parents we have only a limited influence over our children's lives, in fact our influence is enormous. As a parent you will be passing on your philosophy of life both consciously and unconsciously. You will lead the way in showing them how to behave, how to think, how to feel, how to take care of the world they live in. Who you are forms the basis of your child's moral education. Spending some time now thinking about who you are and what is important to you will improve your chances of passing on the values and beliefs which you intended to pass on and in the process, hopefully passing on a world that is fit for future generations.

Select Bibliography

An enormous amount of research has formed the background to this book. These pages represent a selection of the papers and books which readers may find interesting.

Papers and Reports

General

'11th Report on Carcinogens, National Toxicology Program', US Department of Health and Human Services, Public Health Service.

'A case-control study of borderline ovarian tumors: the influence of perineal exposure to talc', Harlow BL and Weiss BS, Am J Epidemiol, 1989; 130: 390–4.

'Acute fluoride toxicity from ingesting home-use dental products in children, birth to 6 years of age', Shulman JD and Wells LM, J Publ Health Dent, 1997; 57: 150–8.

'Acute toxic effects of fragrance products', Anderson RC and Anderson JH, Arch Environ Health, 1998; 53: 138–46.

'Are maternal smoking and stress during pregnancy related to ADHD symptoms in children?' Rodriguez A and Bohlin G, J Child Psychol Psychiatry, 2005; 46(3): 246–54.

'Biology and politics: linking nature and nurture', Masters RD, Ann Rev Polit Sci, 2001; 4: 345–69.

'Blanching and long-term freezing affect various bioactive compounds of vegetables in different ways', Puupponen-Pimiä R, et al, J Sci Food Ag, 2003; 83(14): 1389–1402.

'Breastfeeding and child cognitive development', Kramer MS et al, Arch Gen Psychiatry, 2008; 65(5): 578–84.

'breastfeeding and optimal visual development', Birch E et al, J Pediatr Ophthalmol Strabismus 1993 Jan–Feb; 30(1):33–8.

'Breastfeeding and visual development of children', Chapman J, Hum Lact, 2007; 23: 287–8.

'Breastfeeding in infancy and social mobility: 60-year follow-up of Boyd Orr cohort', Martin RM et al, Arch Dis Child, 2007; 92: 317–21.

'Chemical Hazard Data Availability Study: What Do We Really Know About the Safety of High Production Volume Chemicals?' EPA, 1998.

'Cigarette, alcohol, and caffeine consumption: risk factors for spontaneous abortion', Rasche V et al, Acta Obs Gyn Scand, 2003; 82(2): 182–8.

'Contraception during breastfeeding', Grimes DA, Contraception Report, 2003; 13(4): 7–13.

'Crisis in chemicals: The threat posed by the "biomedical revolution" to the profits, liabilities and regulation of industries making and using chemicals', Friends of the Earth, May 2000.

'Environmental and heritable factors in the causation of cancer – Analyses of cohorts of twins from Sweden, Denmark, and Finland', Lichtenstein, P et al, N Eng J Med, 2000; 343: 78–85.

'Environmental medicine, Part 1: The human burden of environmental toxins and their common health effects', Crinnion WJ, Altern Med Rev, 2000; 5: 52–63.

'Everyday exposure to toxic pollutants', Ott WR, Roberts JW, Sci Am, 1998; Feb: 86–91.

'Exposure to volatile organic compounds in indoor air: A review', Brown SK in Proceedings of the International Clean Air Conference of the Clean Air Society of Australia and New Zealand, 1992; 1: 95–104.

'Fluoride in dental products: safety considerations', Whitford GM, J Dent Res, 1987; 66, 1056–60.

'Genital talc exposure and risk of ovarian cancer', Cramer DW et al, Int J Cancer, 1999; 81: 351–6.

'Health hazard information', US Environmental Protection Agency, 1991.

'How are children different from adults?', Bearer CF, Environ Health Perspect, 1995; 103 (Suppl 6): 7–12.

'How chemical exposures affect reproductive health: Patient fact sheet', Greater Boston Physicians for Social Responsibility, GBPSR, 1996.

'Human health and chemical mixtures: an overview', Carpenter DO et al, Environmental Health Perspectives, 1998; 106 (Suppl 6):1263–70.

'Identification of Polar Volatile Organic Compounds in Consumer Products and Common Microenvironments', Wallace L, EPA, 1991.

'In vitro and in vivo oestrogenicity of UV screens', Schlumpf M et al, Environ Health Perspect, 2001; 109: 239–44.

'Inhalation challenge effects of perfume scent strips in patients with asthma', Kumar P et al, Ann Allergy Asthma Immunol, 1995; 75: 429–33.

'Introduction to hormone disrupting compounds', Warhurst M. Available online at: http://website.lineone.net/~mwarhurst/

'Maternal underweight and the risk of spontaneous abortion', Helgstrand S and Nybo Andersen AM, Acta Obstetrica Gyneacol Scand 2005; 84: 1197–1201.

'Mutagenicity of cosmetic products containing Kathon', Connor TH et al, Environ Mol Mutagen, 1996; 28: 127–32.

'N-Nitrosoalkanolamines in cosmetics in relevance to human cancer of N-nitroso compounds, tobacco smoke and mycotoxins', Eisenbrand G, et al, IARC 1991.

'National Report on Human Exposure to Environmental Chemicals', Centers for Disease Control and Prevention, Atlanta, GA: CDC, March 2001; available online at: www.cdc.gov/nceh/dls/report/

'Neurotoxic fragrance produces ceroid and myelin disease', Spencer PS et al, Science, 1979; 204: 633–5.

'Neurotoxic properties of musk ambrette', Spencer PS et al, Toxicol Appl Pharmacol, 1984; 75: 571–5.

'Obesity is associated with increased first trimester and recurrent miscarriage: matched case-control study', Lashen, H et al, Human Reproduction, 2004; 19(7): 1644–6,

'Ontogeny of foetal exposure to maternal cortisol using midtrimester amniotic fluid as a biomarker', Sarkar P et al, Clinical Endocrinology, 2007; 66 (5), 636–40.

'Our Stolen Future', Colbin T et al, available online at: www.ourstolenfuture.org

'Patch testing with fragrances: results of a multicentre of the European environmental and contact dermatitis research group with 48 frequently used constituents of perfumes', Frosch PJ et al, Contact Dermatitis, 1995; 33: 333–42.

'Personal exposure, indoor-outdoor relationships, and breath levels of toxic air pollutants measured for 355 persons in New Jersey', Wallace LA et al, EPA 0589.

'Personal exposures, outdoor concentrations, and breath levels of toxic air pollutants measured for 425 persons in urban, suburban and rural areas', Wallace LA et al, EPA 0589, presented at the Annual Meeting of Air Pollution Control Association, San Francisco, CA, 25 June 1984.

'Pharmaceuticals and personal care products in the environment: agents of subtle change?' Daughton CG and Ternes TA, Environ Health Perspect, 1999; 107 (Suppl 6): 907–38.

'Phenolic compound contents in edible parts of broccoli inflorescences after domestic cooking', Vallejo F, et al, J Sci Food Ag, 2003; 83(14): 1511–16.

'Prenatal exposure to maternal depression and cortisol influences infant temperament', Davis EP et al, J Am Acad Child Adolesc Psychiatry, 2007; 46(6): 737–46.

'Prospective study of talc use and ovarian cancer', Gertig DM et al, J Natl Cancer Inst, 2000; 92: 249–52.

'Risk factors for first trimester miscarriage – results from a UK-population-based case-control study', Maconochie N et al, Br J Obs Gyn, 2007; 114(2): 170–86.

'Second national report on human exposure to environmental chemicals', Centers for Disease Control and Prevention, Atlanta, GA, March 2003, available online at: www.cdc.gov/exposurereport

'Solvents and neurotoxicity', White RF and Proctor SP, Lancet, 1997; 349: 1239–43.

'Some alkyl hydroxy benzoate preservatives (parabens) are oestrogenic', Routledge EJ et al, Toxicol Applied Pharmacol, 1998; 153: 12–19.

'Synergistic activation of oestrogen receptors with combinations of environmental chemicals', Arnold SF et al, Science, 1996; 272: 1489–92.

'The oestrogenic activity of phthalate esters in vitro', Harris C et al, Environ Health Perspectives, 1997; 105: 802–11.

'The relationship between perineal cosmetic talc usage and ovarian talc particle burden', Heller DS et al, Am J Obstet Gynecol, 1996; 74: 1507–10.

'Toxic effects of air freshener emissions', Anderson RC and Anderson JH, Arch Environ Health, 1997; 52: 433–41.

'Toxic nation: A report on pollution in Canadians', Environmental Defence, Canada Nov 2005 317 Adelaide Street West, Suite 705 Toronto, ON M5V 1P9, see online at: www.environmentaldefence.ca.

'Ultrasound? Unsound', Beech BAL and Robinson J, AIMS, 1996.

Books

1001 Chemicals in Everyday Products, 2nd ed, Grace Ross Lewis, Wiley-Interscience, 1999.

A Guide to Effective Care in Pregnancy and Childbirth, Murray Enkin, et al, Oxford University Press, 2000.

Chemical Exposures: Low Levels and High Stakes, Nicholas Ashford and Claudia Miller, Wiley & Sons, 1998.

Cleaning Yourself to Death, Pat Thomas, New Leaf, 2001.

Clinical Toxicology of Commercial Products, 5th ed, Robert Gosselin et al, Williamson & Wilkins, 1984.

Cosmetics Unmasked, Dr Stephen Antczak and Gina Antczak, Thorsons, 2001.

Entering The World, Michel Odent, Penguin, 1984.

Every Woman's Birthrights, Pat Thomas, Thorsons, 1996.

Every Birth is Different, Pat Thomas, Headline, 1997.

Healing Through Nutrition, Dr Melvyn R Werbach, Thorsons, 1993.

Living Dangerously, Pat Thomas , New Leaf, 2003.

Living Healthy in a Toxic World, David Steinman and Michael R Wisner, Perigree, 1996.

Nutritional Medicine, Dr Stephen Davies, Dr Alan Stewart, Pan, 1987.

'Overview of similarities and differences between children and adults: implications for risk assessment', Roberts RJ, in Guzelian PS et al (eds), Similarities *and Differences Between Children and Adults*, ILSI Press, 1992: 1–15.

Pregnancy: The Common Sense Guide, Pat Thomas, New Leaf, 1999.

Obstetric Myths and Research Realities, Henci Goer, Bergin & Garvey, 1995.

Pursuing the Birth Machine – The Search for Appropriate Birth Technology, Marsden Wagner, ACE Graphics, 1994.

Safer Childbirth? A Critical History of Maternity Care, Marjorie Tew, Free Association Books, 1998.

Secret Ingredients, Peter Cox and Peggy Brusseau, Bantam Books, 1997.

SELECT BIBLIOGRAPHY

The Better Pregnancy Diet, Patrick Holford. London: ION Press, 1993.

The Complete Guide to Household Chemicals, Robert J Palma, Prometheus Books, 1995.

The Precautionary principle in Action – A Handbook, Joel Tickner et al, Science and Environmental Health Network, 1998.

The Safe Shopper's Bible – A Consumer's Guide to Nontoxic Household Products, David Steinman and Samuel Epstein, Macmillan, 1995.

Understanding Diagnostic Tests in the Childbearing Year: A holistic Guide to Evaluating the Health of Mother and Baby, Anne Frye, Labrys Press, 2007.

Unreasonable Risk, Samuel Epstein, Environmental Toxicology, Inc, 2001.

What's in this Stuff?, Pat Thomas, Rodale, 2006

Appendix 1
Essential Nutrients

Vitamins

Vitamin A
- **Function:** Antioxidant and immune system booster. Essential for night vision. Promotes healthy skin, keeps outer layers of tissue and organs healthy.
- **Best Natural Sources:** Fish liver oil, liver, green and yellow vegetables, eggs, milk and dairy, yellow fruits.

B1 (thiamine)
- **Function:** Aids digestion and is essential for energy production. Keeps nervous system, muscles and heart functioning normally.
- **Best Natural Sources:** Yeast, rice husks, whole wheat, oatmeal, peanuts, pork, most vegetables, bananas, milk.

B2 (riboflavin)
- **Function:** Aids the metabolism of carbohydrates, fats and proteins. Necessary to repair and maintain healthy skin, nails and hair. Helps regulate body acidity.

- **Best Natural Sources:** Milk, liver, kidney, yeast, cheese, leafy green vegetables, fish, eggs.

B3 (niacin)
- **Function:** Essential for energy production and brain function. Helps balance blood sugar and cholesterol levels. Promotes healthy skin. Can help prevent headaches.
- **Best Natural Sources:** Liver, mushrooms, tuna, chicken, salmon, lamb, asparagus, cabbage, mackerel, turkey, tomatoes, courgettes, squash, cauliflower, wholewheat products, brewer's yeast, kidney, wheat germ, fish, eggs, roasted peanuts, avocados, dates, figs, prunes.

B5 (pantothenic acid)
- **Function:** Essential for brain and nerves. Aids energy production and fat metabolism. Combats stress. Maintains healthy skin and hair. Meat, wholegrains, wheat germ, bran, kidney, liver, heart, green vegetables, brewer's yeast, nuts, chicken, molasses.

B6 (pyridoxine)
- **Function:** Aids digestion, brain function and hormone production. Helps balance sex hormones. Natural antidepressant and diuretic. Alleviates nausea and muscle cramps.
- **Best Natural Sources:** Watercress, bananas, squash, broccoli, cauliflower, asparagus, lentils, red kidney beans, onions, brewer's yeast, wheat bran, wheat germ, liver, kidney, heart, cantaloupe, cabbage, molasses, milk, eggs, beef, seeds and nuts.

B12 (cyanocobalamin)
- **Function:** Helps the body utilise proteins. Necessary for energy production. Helps prevent anaemia. Improves concentration, memory and balance. Combats stress.
- **Best Natural Sources:** Oysters, sardines, lamb, prawns, cottage cheese, poultry, cheese, liver, beef, pork, eggs, milk, kidney.

Biotin
- **Function:** Helps the body use essential fats. Promotes healthy skin, hair and nerves. Eases muscle pains.

- **Best Natural Sources:** Peas, tomatoes, cauliflower, lettuce, grapefruit, watermelon, sweetcorn, almonds, fruit, brewer's yeast, beef, liver, eggs, milk, kidney, unpolished rice.

Folic acid (folacin)
- **Function:** Essential for brain and nerve function. Taken preconceptually and in early pregnancy, can help prevent neural tube defects. Helps prevent anaemia and can protect against intestinal parasites and food poisoning.
- **Best Natural Sources:** Dark green leafy vegetables, carrots, yeast, peanuts, sesame seeds, hazelnuts, walnuts, liver, egg yolk, melon, apricots, pumpkin, avocado, beans, whole wheat and dark rye flour.

Vitamin C (ascorbic acid)
- **Function:** Antioxidant and immune system booster. Fights stress. Heals wounds, A natural laxative. Improves elasticity of the skin. Necessary for a healthy heart.
- **Best Natural Sources:** Citrus fruits, peppers, watercress, berries, lemons, kiwi, melon, green leafy vegetables, tomatoes, cauliflower, potato and sweet potato.

Vitamin D (ergocalciferol, cholecalciferol)
- **Function:** Helps the body utilise calcium and maintain strong bones. Can help in the treatment of conjunctivitis. Taken with A and C can boost immune system function.
- **Best Natural Sources:** Oily fish such as herring, mackerel, salmon and sardines, milk, cottage cheese, oysters, eggs.

Vitamin E (d-alpha tocopherol)
- **Function:** Antioxidant. Helps the body use oxygen. Keeps heart and circulatory system healthy. Improves skin and hastens wound healing. Aids fertility. Alleviates fatigue.
- **Best Natural Sources:** Unrefined sunflower and corn oils, wheat germ, soya beans, salmon, tuna, sardines, peanuts, broccoli, Brussels sprouts, sweet potatoes, leafy green vegetables, seeds, pulses, enriched flour, whole wheat, wholegrain cereals, eggs.

EFAs (essential fatty acids: omega 3 and omega 6)
- **Function:** Necessary for brain and nerve function. Has a role in preventing pre-eclampsia. Lowers cholesterol. Improves heart function.
- **Best Natural Sources:** Vegetable oils (wheat germ, linseed, sunflower, safflower, soya and peanut), peanuts, sunflower seeds, pumpkins seeds, hemp seeds, sesame seeds, walnuts, pecans, almonds, avocados, oily fish.

Vitamin K (phylloquinone)
- **Function:** Controls blood clotting.
- **Best Natural Sources:** Leafy green vegetables, potatoes, watercress, peas, beans, yogurt, alfalfa, egg yolk, sunflower oil, soya bean oil, fish liver oils, kelp.

Minerals

Calcium
- **Function:** Necessary for a healthy heart, nerves and muscles. Improves skin, bone and teeth health. Can relieve aching muscles and reduce cramping. Maintains the acid-alkaline balance of the body.
- **Best Natural Sources:** Milk and milk products, all cheeses, brewer's yeast, prunes, corn tortillas, parsley, soya beans, sardines, tinned salmon, peanuts, walnuts, sunflower seeds, dried beans, green vegetables.

Chromium
- **Function:** Balances blood sugar levels, normalises hunger and reduces cravings. Essential for a healthy heart.
- **Best Natural Sources:** Brewer's yeast, wholemeal and rye bread, green peppers, parsnips, cornmeal, lamb, potatoes, oysters, eggs, chicken, corn oil, clams.

Iron
- **Function:** Prevents anaemia and fatigue. Improves skin tone. Promotes resistance to disease and aids wound healing.

- **Best Natural Sources:** Pork, liver, beef, kidney, heart and liver, dried peaches, red meat, egg yolk, oysters, nuts and seeds, raisins, beans, asparagus, molasses, oatmeal.

Magnesium
- **Function:** Essential for energy production. Strengthens bones and teeth. Promotes healthy muscles including the heart muscle and, in pregnancy, the uterus. Maintains a healthy nervous system.
- **Best Natural Sources:** Nuts, dates, figs, lemons, grapefruit, yellow corn, seeds, dark green vegetables, apples.

Manganese
- **Function:** Necessary for healthy bones, cartilage, tissue and nerves. Helps alleviate fatigue. Stabilises blood sugar. Required for proper brain function.
- **Best Natural Sources:** Grapes, nuts, watercress, pineapple, okra, endive, celery, berries, lima beans, beetroot, green leafy vegetables, peas, beets, egg yolk, wholegrain cereals.

Molybdenum
- **Function:** Helps the body to eliminate waste products. Helps prevent anaemia.
- **Best Natural Sources:** Tomatoes, wheat germ, pork, lentils, beans, dark green leafy vegetables, wholegrains.

Phosphorus
- **Function:** Builds muscle tissue. Aids lactation. Maintains bone and teeth health. Aids energy production and metabolism.
- **Best Natural Sources:** Present in most foods.

Potassium
- **Function:** Helps in the elimination of waste products. Maintains the body's fluid balance. Promotes healthy nerves and muscles. Involved in metabolism and maintaining blood sugar levels.
- **Best Natural Sources:** Citrus fruits, watercress, all green leafy vegetables, mint leaves, sunflower seeds, bananas, potatoes, mushrooms, cauliflower, pumpkin, courgettes.

Selenium

- **Function:** Antioxidant. Reduces inflammation. Promotes healthy heart. Needed for metabolism.
- **Best Natural Sources:** Tuna, oysters, molasses, cottage cheese, mushrooms, herring, wheat germ, bran, onions, tomatoes, broccoli, courgette.

Sodium

- **Function:** Maintains the body's water balance. Necessary for nerve and muscle function.
- **Best Natural Sources:** Salt, olives, prawns, miso, celery, beetroot, crab, ham, bacon, shellfish, carrots, beets, artichokes, dried beef, brain, kidney.

Zinc

- **Function:** Important for healing, essential for growth. Controls hormones which are messengers from the reproductive organs. Relieves stress. Aids bone and teeth formation. Essential for energy production. Boosts immunity.
- **Best Natural Sources:** Ginger root, beef, lamb, pork, wheat germ, brewer's yeast, prawns, pumpkin seeds, nuts, eggs, turnips, oats, dry split peas, ground mustard.

Note: Liver is a rich source of nutrients but can also concentrate toxins and heavy metals. Because of its high vitamin-A (retinol) content (and the association of high levels of vitamin-A intake with foetal abnormalities), liver consumption should be restricted or avoided during pregnancy. The occasional serving of organic liver is unlikely to be harmful, however, consider the following guidelines:

- Liver-based foods (minced liver patties and liver steaks, liver stew, baked liver casserole) should be avoided during the whole pregnancy.
- The amount of liver sausage and liver pâté consumed during pregnancy should not exceed 200g (7oz) a week. No more than 100g (3½oz) should be consumed at any one time.
- If liver sausage or liver pâté are being consumed daily, their use should

be limited to a maximum of 30g (1oz) a day. In practice this corresponds to about two slices of liver sausage or 2 tablespoons of liver pâté.

If in doubt, always consult your midwife or physician.

Appendix 2

Natural Help for Pregnancy 'Symptoms'

Once pregnancy is confirmed, a woman enters arguably one of the most exciting periods of her life, and one in which she may become more body aware than ever before. Many women are surprised to find that almost no part of their body remains unchanged by pregnancy. Some of these changes such as dry eyes, sinusitis and tingling fingers and legs, are temporary. Others, like stretch marks, will be with you for life.

The sort of normal changes associated with pregnancy will vary from woman to woman. Reactions to body changes can also vary. What causes concern in one woman may be nothing more than a mild inconvenience to another. What they all have in common is their normality and frequency.

The fact that such changes are normal, however, is of little consolation if you are feeling ill and uncomfortable. Happily, there is much you can do on your own to help relieve uncomfortable symptoms. Where possible, the general advice here should be used in conjunction with any alternative method you choose. Also, remember that many of the symptoms you experience will be less intense if you are able to make the time to rest during each day. This is especially true during the first few months of pregnancy when nausea and fatigue are a common occurrence.

Backache

As pregnancy progresses, the additional weight you are carrying can put your lower back under stress. Over the months, your pelvic joints will be loosening up in order to facilitate labour and the structure which normally supports your back becomes less stable and less supportive. In addition to spinal pain, some women also experience sharp pains that begin in their sacroiliac joints (the joints which lie on either side of your tailbone) and shoot right down the leg, making walking and moving difficult.

Stay off your feet when you can. Sacroiliac pain can feel worse when you lie on your back so try resting in a different position, well supported by pillows if necessary. Back pain can also be the result of postural problems. Some find the progressive shift in their centre of gravity hard to adapt to and end up arching their backs and thrusting their bellies out to compensate. Pay regular attention to how you are standing and sitting and try to keep your pelvis tucked under you.

A good exercise for this is the pelvic tilt. To do this, lie on the floor with your legs bent, breathe in and as you exhale press the small of your back against the floor. Once you've mastered this movement, practising the same thing standing up will help improve your posture. In addition, when you can, avoid high-heeled shoes which will only make maintaining a stable posture more difficult.

Bleeding

Slight bleeding or spotting during pregnancy does not necessarily indicate a miscarriage. Around 10 per cent of women will experience some bleeding during the first 28 weeks of pregnancy, and slightly fewer after that time. When it does occur it can often be linked to the time when you would normally be having a period. Bleeding may also occur around 14 weeks when the placenta takes over hormone production from the corpus luteum (the part of the ovary which produces several different hormones including progesterone, which stimulates the lining of the uterus to grow).

Less common is the bleeding from an ectopic pregnancy. In an ectopic pregnancy the embryo gets 'lost' and implants itself elsewhere than the uterus, usually one of the Fallopian tubes. This potentially more dangerous bleed usually occurs around 6– 12 weeks and is accompanied by one-sided abdominal pain. Bleeding is caused by a rupture of the tubes and must be addressed with surgery to terminate the pregnancy and repair the tube.

After 28 weeks, bleeding and pain can be caused by the placenta prematurely peeling away from the uterine wall. This rare condition is known as placental abruption and is accompanied by continuous pain. You will be losing blood internally, so if you suspect this get to the hospital immediately since your baby's and your own life will be at risk.

Finally, bleeding very near to term can occur if you have *placenta praevia* – where the placenta is covering the cervix. As the cervix dilates (and this process can begin before labour) the placenta can be torn. Because of this, women with *placenta praevia* are often advised to have a caesarean before term, although this is not always necessary.

There is not much you can do about any of these types of bleeding. Doctors often advise that early bleeds require complete rest. Rest and contemplation are an important way to deal with the profound emotions caused by an early bleed, however there is little reliable evidence that resting will avert a possible miscarriage. If you are more comfortable being on your feet and going about your business you should be able to make this choice without being made to feel guilty.

Candida

Fungal infections (also known as thrush or yeast infections) can be aggravated by the hormonal changes of pregnancy that alter the acid/alkali balance of your vagina.

It is normal to experience increased vaginal secretions during pregnancy, but if your vulva becomes red and irritated and you have a white, cottage cheese-like discharge, it is a sign of vaginal candida. It is best to clear this condition during pregnancy since your baby can become infected at birth.

Antifungal pessaries and creams will be ineffective after a while so instead of treating the symptom, treat the cause. Possible triggers include overuse of antibiotics, stress and previous use of the birth-control pill, but the strongest link is with diet. If you are prone to candida infections it is particularly important that you remove all acidic and sugary foods and refined carbohydrates from your diet. In some women, dairy products are also a trigger. Instead, make sure your diet is based on wholefoods and includes plenty of immunity-boosting garlic, onions, turnips, cabbage and plain, live yogurt.

Candida loves warm, moist atmospheres, so wear loose cotton underwear, which allows air to circulate. If you regularly use bubble baths, stop. They will irritate the area further (and are implicated in recurrent urinary tract infections in mothers and babies). Also, no douching (never in pregnancy) or vaginal deodorants and switch to white, unscented toilet paper.

Early signs of vaginal candida can be treated with plain, live yogurt. Before going to bed, insert a few teaspoons into the vagina. Repeat this each evening until the symptoms improve. Caught early enough, the friendly bacteria in the yogurt will multiply, devouring the candida. Calendula cream or tincture will help ease external irritation. In addition, you might persuade your partner to be tested for candida since you can become reinfected through sexual contact.

Constipation

Hormonal changes during pregnancy will make food move more slowly through your digestive system. Although generally hormonal in origin, constipation can be made a great deal worse by a poor diet. Stress can also make it worse and if your symptoms are really severe, it may be worth considering whether you have a food allergy or intolerance. Constipation can also be caused by iron supplements.

Instead of laxatives, increase your intake of fibre. Not the kind you find in wheat bran, but the more bowel-friendly kind you find in raw vegetables, fruits, oat bran and rice. This fibre is water-soluble and will aid the passage of foods through the gut. Wheat bran is an irritant and, because it is not water soluble, it can make your stools dry and harder to pass. For breakfast, try including fruits such as figs and prunes – but not the processed kind that can be high in sugar.

Drink plenty of fluids – the more you drink, the more efficient your system will become at flushing out toxins and other impurities. Try drinking a cup of hot water flavoured with a squeeze of lemon juice just before, or with your meal. If this does not appeal, try a herbal tea such as camomile, fennel or ginger. Eating small, unhurried meals throughout the day will help your system process food more efficiently.

Massaging your belly in a clockwise direction is also helpful. Gentle massage (with or without aromatherapy oils) can be carried out by yourself or your partner and can be very pleasant as well as effective.

Cramps

You can get muscle cramps almost anywhere in your body during pregnancy but the most common site is the calves. Often these painful spasms seem to come out of nowhere and although individual spasms may only last a short time, they can be very severe. For quick relief, stretch the muscle by extending your heel and bringing your toes towards you.

Cramp can be the result of the extra weight you are carrying. Stretching in bed in the morning and pointing your toes can also bring on quite severe muscle spasms. Cramps may also be caused by salt or calcium deficiency and circulation changes, so the best prevention is to make sure that you take regular exercise and watch your nutrient intake. Your diet should include plenty of calcium- and magnesium-rich foods (see Appendix 1) and you should add salt to taste.

Cystitis

This urinary infection can strike quite suddenly and is caused by an inflammation of the bladder. You will know when you have it because urinating can become excruciating, producing a burning pain, and you will have the urge to pee even if there is nothing in your bladder.

Cystitis can occur alongside other vaginal infections such as candida. Since both are linked strongly with diet, you should investigate food allergies as a possible cause.

You can prevent attacks by wearing cotton underwear and not getting too chilly. Avoid spicy and sugary foods and alcohol. Drinking unsweetened cranberry juice is very helpful. If you cannot find this, try some of the other cranberry-based remedies available in healthfood shops. Your best option during an attack, however, is to drink plenty of water. Putting a teaspoon of bicarbonate of soda in your glass of water will help relieve symptoms.

If you take early action, you will probably be able to avoid antibiotics. However, if you do need to resort to antibiotics, make sure you take supplemental probiotics, such as *acidophilous* and *bifidobacteria*, at the same time and eat lots of plain, live yogurt.

Fatigue

No matter how energetic you are, at some point pregnancy will take its toll on your energy levels. There is no complicated remedy for exhaustion. When you are tired you must rest. In the end, the best way to prevent exhaustion is to listen to your body and learn your new limits.

As pregnancy progresses you may find it more difficult to sleep. Finding a comfortable position may be difficult and you may need to get up frequently to urinate. Aches and pains may bother you more and interrupted sleep can result in extreme fatigue. Tiredness can also be linked to your emotional state, for instance if you feel anxious or depressed.

Developing new ways of approaching rest and relaxation will help. Taking cat naps during the day will make a big difference to your energy levels – it will also get you in a good habit for after birth, when you will need to rest when the baby rests.

Being physically run down can produce fatigue, so in addition to regular periods of rest, make sure you are eating well. Avoid junk food, especially those high in sugar and caffeine. Regular exercise can actually help relieve tiredness and aerobic exercise is a particularly good choice.

Fluid retention

Water retention in pregnancy is common and, on its own, rarely a sign that anything is wrong. Only when it is combined with high blood pressure and protein in the urine is it a possible sign of pre-eclampsia. Water retention is especially noticeable late in pregnancy when you may find that your rings and bracelets no longer fit properly.

Hot weather, prolonged standing and fatigue can make puffiness in the fingers, ankles, calves, feet and face more pronounced. One side effect of water retention is carpal tunnel syndrome. This is when increased supply of fluids to the extremities causes swelling and pressure on the nerves and blood vessels that pass through the wrist canal (known as the carpal tunnel). When this happens you may experience numbness, tingling and even pain in the hand, fingers and sometimes the arm. The condition usually improves after the birth.

Your body needs the extra water volume to cope with all the extra substances which are floating around in it (such as waste products created by your baby) so don't take diuretics. Your kidneys are under enough strain already and these will only cause problems. A good wholefood diet and regular exercise will promote the elimination of excess water and help reduce puffiness. You will also need to make sure you get plenty of rest each day. Try supplementing your diet with natural diuretics such as garlic, raw onions, apples, red grapes or grape juice.

Carpal tunnel syndrome can be worse in the morning due to fluids accumulating in your hands overnight. Try holding your arms over your head for a short while to drain off excess fluids. Gentle massage to the wrists and hands will also help ease the pain.

Headache

Pregnancy does not raise your risk of developing headaches. However, since a number of women feel under a greater amount of stress at this time, stress-related headaches are not uncommon. Headaches are also more likely on hot days when the extra weight and the extra blood you are carrying will make it harder for you to keep cool. Ironically, some women who suffer from regular migraines find that their headaches disappear during pregnancy!

The best way to deal with headaches is to do all you can to prevent them occurring. Try to anticipate stress at home and in the workplace and where possible, do what you can to limit your exposure to stressful situations. Learn to listen to your body and when it says you have had enough, stop. Pregnancy can exaggerate adverse reactions to some foods – if you are able to link your headaches to a type of food it is best to remove it from your diet.

Heartburn

Another effect of increased circulating hormones in your body is the softening of the valve between the oesophagus and stomach. When this happens, foods and gastric acids can be regurgitated. These can irritate the lining of the oesophagus, causing a feeling of pain and a sharp burning sensation in the chest. As your uterus grows it can aggravate things further by putting pressure on your stomach. Heartburn can follow a rushed meal; it can also follow an emotional upset. Food allergies are also a potential cause.

Eating small, frequent meals is a good idea. The wisdom of this will become more apparent as you get bigger and your stomach gets squeezed into a smaller space. Don't eat too late at night – give yourself at least two hours to digest your evening meal. Digestion begins in the mouth, so relieve the burden on your stomach by chewing your food well.

The kinds of food you eat may also be important. Cut out spicy, greasy, sugary or acidic foods. Some women find that not drinking with a meal helps, since sometimes this can dilute digestive juices. Instead, try sipping a herbal tea such as fennel after a meal to aid digestion but stay away from coffee and tea since this can increase stomach acidity.

Insomnia

Your sleep patterns will change during pregnancy and the occasional sleepless night is not uncommon, especially late in pregnancy. If insomnia becomes a regular feature of your pregnancy, however, your health will begin to suffer, so it is best to get to the bottom of whatever is keeping you awake.

Often the cause is emotional. During a busy work day you may not have time to think about impending parenthood and how it will affect your life. At night, when things are quiet, you may find that worries crowd your mind. You may feel depressed and anxious and all these feelings can interfere with your ability to drop off to sleep.

Try to avoid sleeping pills, which do not benefit you or your baby. Talking to someone – your partner, a self-help group, your midwife or a counsellor – is the best way to deal with the worries that keep you awake.

If you feel physically uncomfortable and this is keeping you awake, try one or more of the following suggestions. Get creative with the pillows on the bed. If necessary, invest in a few more so you can prop various parts of your body up at night. As pregnancy progresses you may feel hotter so make sure the room is well ventilated.

Although you should not eat a main meal too close to bedtime, a light snack just before retiring can help you avoid night-time hypoglycaemia. The brain needs a constant supply of glucose even at rest and a drop in blood sugar signals the body to produce chemicals that stimulate sugar release. The resulting rise in blood sugar can actually wake you up. Finally, regular exercise – but not just before retiring – can improve the quality and duration of sleep.

Morning sickness

Feelings of nausea, occasional vomiting, tiredness and lethargy are as common as they are uncomfortable. For most women, these symptoms disappear after the first few months. However, for some, especially those expecting twins, they may last throughout pregnancy.

There are many contributing factors to nausea during pregnancy. Some are physical: low blood sugar, low blood pressure, hormonal changes, nutritional deficiency (especially in vitamin B6 and iron), or nutritional excess (especially spicy, sugary and refined foods). If nausea reappears during the last few weeks of pregnancy it can be because the growing uterus is putting pressure on the stomach. But there is also an emotional side to nausea. Women who are carrying unwanted babies, or who feel in some way resentful about the pregnancy seem to experience nausea more severely than those who do not.

Nausea accompanied by relentless vomiting requires medical help since this can dehydrate and deprive the woman of essential nutrients. Otherwise, try these self-help measures:

- Try taking two or three teaspoons of apple cider vinegar (not any other kind) in warm water first thing in the morning.
- Make a warming tea by pouring boiling water over a teaspoon of freshly grated ginger root. Sweeten with honey if you prefer. If you are out of the house and can't brew up, any food item containing ginger should help. Some women swear by stale ginger ale, others prefer the crystallised ginger available in some specialist cooking shops. Still others use it liberally in cooking in both sweet and savoury dishes.
- Acupressure can be very effective. Studies show that pressure on the pericardium 6 (P6) point can provide relatively quick relief from nausea, though it may not help to reduce vomiting. To find this point place your hand palm-up and measure two thumb-widths above the most prominent wrist crease; P6 is just above this point, in line with the middle finger. Some chemists sell wrist bands which stimulate the P6 point and claim to help relieve nausea. These have been shown to work for some women.
- Numerous studies have shown that deficiency in vitamin B6 is at the root of many cases of nausea. Try taking at least 25–50mg daily as part of a B-complex supplement.

Nosebleeds

Spontaneous nosebleeds are the result of the greater amount of blood circulating in your body. They may come on when you feel particularly stressed since your blood pressure will also rise during these times. The condition usually improves after birth.

In the meantime, they can be stopped by using a cold compress on the bridge of your nose while keeping your head back. Some women find that a small amount of Vaseline rubbed inside of the nostril helps stop the bleeding. Try to avoid blowing your nose too hard as this can also bring on a bleed.

Restless legs

This is an uncomfortable condition that produces a strange crawling sensation in the legs, rather like having an electric current running through them. It occurs mostly in the early evening and at night when you are resting, making your legs feel uncontrollably jittery, giving you an irresistible urge to move around. Restless Leg Syndrome can make relaxation and even sleep difficult since it produces repeated and uncontrollable leg shakes. The condition usually disappears after birth.

There are several contributory factors to this condition. Hypoglycaemia is one and over consumption of caffeine is another. The combination of the two has been shown to make symptoms worse. Anaemia is a factor so make sure you eat plenty of iron-rich foods. Adequate levels of folic acid and vitamin E may also be helpful. Some people find that regular exercise helps alleviate the condition. Warm baths before retiring are also helpful.

Sinus congestion

Sinusitis in pregnancy can often be caused by a swelling of the mucous membrane inside the nostrils and sinuses. For some women, especially in later pregnancy, the condition can become chronic.

Sinus problems usually improve after birth but in the meantime you may have to learn to breathe through your mouth. If this makes your mouth feel dry, especially at night, keep a glass or bottle of water handy and take frequent sips. Try also keeping your lips moisturised with lip balm or cream. Sometimes nasal congestion is associated with food allergies and a good nutritionist will be able to guide you in this matter.

In the meantime you might also want to consider cutting down on foods which can increase nasal secretions such as dairy products. Although these are often considered essential in pregnancy there are other good sources of protein and calcium which will ensure that you are adequately nourished while relieving pressure on your sinuses (see Appendix 1).

Stretch marks

Some women get stretch marks and some don't. Although it is more common in women of Celtic extraction, there appears to be little rhyme or reason for their appearance. They are not necessarily linked with weight gain, there is very little convincing evidence that there is much you can do to prevent them appearing and once they have appeared you can't simply rub them away with creams.

Whenever your body gets bigger faster than your skin can adapt, stretch marks will appear. Pregnant women are not the only ones who get them; they are quite common, for instance, in both male and female body builders. Although they fade over time and are non-threatening to a woman's health, many women feel deeply emotional about their stretch marks. The more you feel that pregnancy shouldn't change your life, the more stretch marks seem to mock you and remind you that your body and your life have changed permanently. Accept them, and take what few steps you can to limit their appearance.

Steady weight gain throughout pregnancy will take the strain off your skin. Make sure your diet is rich in vitamins C and E – both essential for maintaining skin tone. Some women swear by cocoa butter and there are a number of good formulations on the market. It is unclear whether a special stretch mark formula is genuinely better than a simple, solid cocoa butter preparation. Lotions will feel lighter on the skin but solid cocoa butter has the advantage of providing a wax-like barrier which locks moisture into the skin. Vitamin E oil rubbed daily into the abdomen, breasts and thighs may also be of benefit.

Varicose veins and haemorrhoids (piles)

Increased blood volume during pregnancy puts your veins are under pressure. In addition, hormonal changes relax the muscular walls of the blood vessels. This action makes it more difficult for your veins to move blood from the lower body back to the heart. The increasing weight of your uterus will put more stress on the pelvic veins and if you are experiencing constipation this can also interfere with your pelvic circulation. As a result blood may pool in the lower body and you may get bulging, painful varicose veins on the legs, vulva or rectum.

Varicosities tend to run in families. Pregnant women who have to stand for long periods of time (for instance at work), who sit for long periods during the day and those expecting twins may also get them. Varicosities of the vulva will usually disappear after birth. Those in the anus or legs may or may not improve depending on what action you take to prevent or relieve them during pregnancy.

Avoid constipation, and exercise regularly to improve your circulation. Rest with your legs up as often as you can and when seated avoid crossing your legs. Wear support stockings and avoid squatting or standing for long periods of time.

To reduce swelling, try a cold compress or ice pack on the affected area(s). Likewise, a cool sitz bath (a shallow bath which just reaches your legs and/or bottom) may help improve circulation.

The way your child is born will also affect whether or not piles improve – a good reason to avoid strenuous pushing (the baby will come out without it), forceps and ventouse deliveries.

Resources

Pregnancy and Birth

General

Active Birth Centre
www.activebirthcentre.com

Association for Improvements in the Maternity Services (AIMS)
www.aims.org.uk

Caesarean and VBAC (Vaginal Birth After Caesarean) Support
http://caesarean.org.uk

Caesarean Support Network
http://ukselfhelp.info/caesarean

Independent Midwives Association
www.independentmidwives.org.uk

National Childbirth Trust (NCT)
www.nctpregnancyandbabycare.com

Special needs

Alcoholics Anonymous (AA)
www.alcoholics-anonymous.org.uk

BLISS
Support and advice for families of babies born too soon, too small or too sick to cope on their own
www.bliss.org.uk

Emma's Diary
General pregnancy advice
www.emmasdiary.co.uk

Narcotics Anonymous
www.ukna.org

Pre-Eclampsia Society (PETS)
www.pre-eclampsia-society.org.uk

Quit
Advice and support to help you stop
smoking at any time of life
www.quit.org.uk

Relate: Marriage Guidance
www.relate.org.uk

**Stillbirth and Neonatal Death
Society (SANDS)**
www.uk-sands.org

**Twins and Multiple Births
Association (TAMBA)**
www.tamba.org.uk

Postnatal support

**Association of Breastfeeding
Mothers**
www.abm.me.uk

CRY-SIS
Support for families with excessively
crying, sleepless and demanding babies
www.cry-sis.org.uk

Gingerbread
Support for lone parents and their
children
www.gingerbread.org.uk

La Leche League (Great Britain)
Mother-to-mother breastfeeding
support
www.laleche.org.uk

Meet-a-Mum Association (MAMA)
www.mama.co.uk

National Childminding Association
www.ncma.org.uk

Products

General stockists
Companies whose products include
nappies (cloth and eco-disposable),
clothing, food, toiletries, pregnancy
accessories, slings, bedding, nursery
furniture, toys and games.

Baby O
www.baby-o.co.uk

Beaming Baby
www.beamingbaby.co.uk

Born
www.borndirect.com

Cuddlebabes
www.cuddlebabes.co.uk

RESOURCES

Ecotopia
www.ecotopia.co.uk

Ethos
www.ethosbaby.com

Globalkids
www.globalkids.co.uk

Green Baby
www.greenbaby.co.uk

Greenfibres
www.greenfibres.com

Hejhog
www.hejhog.co.uk

Huggababy
www.huggababy.co.uk

Kitty Kins
www.kittykins.co.uk

Little Green Earthlets
www.earthlets.co.uk

Mini Organic
www.mini-organic.co.uk

Natural Collection
www.naturalcollection.com

Natural Nursery
www.naturalnursery.co.uk

Nature's Fibres
www.naturesfibres.com

See Saw
www.seesawtoys.co.uk

Smile Child
www.smilechild.co.uk

So Organic
www.soorganic.com

Spirit of Nature
www.spiritofnature.co.uk

Baby bottles (BPA-free)

Emil
www.spiritofnature.co.uk

Baby Nova
www.greenbabyco.com

Born Free
www.babybornfree.co.uk

Dr Browns
www.drbrowns.co.uk

Medela
www.medela.co.uk

Nappies

National Association of Nappy Services
www.changeanappy.co.uk

Women's Environmental Network (WEN)
www.wen.org.uk/nappies

Cloth nappies

Cut 4 Cloth
www.cut4cloth.co.uk

Ethos
www.ethosbaby.com

Lollipop
www.teamlollipop.co.uk

Natural Child
www.naturalnappies.co.uk

Nappy Tales
www.nappytales.freeserve.co.uk

Sam I Am
www.nappies.net

Snazzypants
www.snazzypants.co.uk

The Nappy Lady
www.thenappylady.co.uk

The Nice Nappy Company
www.nicenappy.co.uk

Twinkle Twinkle
www.twinkleontheweb.co.uk

Eco-disposables and wipes

Moltex Nappies
www.spiritofnature.co.uk

Natural Baby Company
www.naturalbabycompany.com

Naturebotts
www.naturebotts.co.uk

The Nappy Lady
www.thenappylady.co.uk

Tushies
www.tushies.co.uk

Laundry services

Dinky Diapers
Bristol and Bath
www.dinkydiapers.co.uk

Nappy Ever After
Central and North London
www.nappyeverafter.co.uk

Nappy Tales
Oxfordshire
www.nappytales.freeserve.co.uk

Natural Nappies
Essex, Suffolk, Cambridgeshire and
North London
www.naturalnappies.co.uk

Nifty Nappies
North and East Hampshire, West Surrey
and the Berkshire borders
www.niftynappies.co.uk

The Nappy Box
North and West Yorkshire
www.thenappybox.co.uk

The Scottish Nappy Company
Ayrshire, Renfrewshire and Inverclyde
www.scottishnappy.co.uk

Clothes

Adili Ltd
www.adili.com

AraVore
www.aravore-babies.com

Baby O
www.baby-o.co.uk

Beaming Baby
www.beamingbaby.co.uk

Bishopston Trading Company
www.bishopstontrading.co.uk

Bella Natura
www.bellanatura.co.uk

Born
www.borndirect.com

Clean Slate Clothing
www.cleanslateclothing.co.uk

Cut 4 Cloth
www.cut4cloth.co.uk

Fox Fibre
www.vreseis.com

Globalkids
www.globalkids.co.uk

Gossypium
www.gossypium.co.uk

Green Baby
www.greenbaby.co.uk

Greenfibres
www.greenfibres.com

Hejhog
www.hejhog.co.uk

Greensleeves
www.greensleevesclothing.com

Ethical Babe
www.ethicalbabe.com

Huggababy
www.huggababy.co.uk

Kitty Kins
www.kittykins.co.uk

Little Green Earthlets
www.earthlets.co.uk

Mini Organic
www.mini-organic.co.uk

Natural Nursery
www.naturalnursery.co.uk

Nature's Fibres
www.naturesfibres.com

People Tree
www.ptree.co.uk

Natural Clothing
www.naturalclothing.co.uk

Smile Child
www.smilechild.co.uk

Tatty Bumpkin
www.tattybumpkin.com

Baby toiletries

Adili
www.adili.com

Akamuti
www.akamuti.co.uk

Aromakids
www.aromakids.com

Aubrey Organics
www.aubreyorganicsuk.co.uk

Burt's Bees
www.myburtsbees.co.uk

Earth Friendly Baby
www.earth-friendly-baby.co.uk

Earthbound Organics
www.earthbound.co.uk

Essential Care
www.essential-care.co.uk

Green Baby
www.greenbaby.co.uk

Green People
www.greenpeople.co.uk

Lavera
www.lavera.co.uk

My Being Well
www.mybeingwell.com

Neal's Yard Remedies
www.nealsyardremedies.com

Pure Nuff Stuff
www.purenuffstuff.co.uk

Simply Gentle (cotton wool pads)
www.simplygentle.com

So Organic
www.soorganic.com

Spiezia
www.spieziaorganics.com

Tautropfen (baby oil and balm)
www.greenfibres.com

Tisserand
www.tisserand.com

The Organic Pharmacy
www.theorganicpharmacy.com

Trevarno
www.trevarnoskincare.co.uk

Verde
www.verde.co.uk

Weleda
www.weleda.co.uk

Wild Wood Groves
www.wildwoodgroves.com

Eco paints

Auro Organic Paints
www.auroorganic.co.uk

Livos Paints
www.ecomerchant.co.uk

Earthborn Paints
www.earthbornpaints.co.uk

Earth & Reed
www.earth-and-reed.co.uk

Aquamajin
www.constructionresources.com

Biofa
www.greenbuildingstore.co.uk

Nutshell Natural Paints
www.nutshellpaints.com

Fleeces

Little Green Earthlets
www.earthlets.co.uk

Huggababy
www.huggababy.co.uk

Toys

Baby-O
www.baby-o.co.uk

Born
www.borndirect.com

British Toymakers Guild
www.toymakersguild.co.uk

Dawson & Son Wooden Toys
www.dawson-and-son.com

Ecotopia
www.ecotopia.co.uk

Escor Toys
www.escortoys.com

Green Baby
www.greenbaby.co.uk

Green Board Game Company
www.greenboardgames.com

Hejhog
www.hejhog.co.uk

Holz Toys
www.holz-toys.co.uk

In2play
www.in2play.co.uk

Lanka Kade
www.lankakade.co.uk

Myriad
www.myriadonline.co.uk

Spirit of Nature
www.spiritofnature.co.uk

Tatty Bumpkin
www.tattybumpkin.com

Toys for Children
www.woodentoysforchildren.co.uk

Toyworm
www.toyworm.co.uk

Tulip Toys
www.tuliptoys.co.uk

Slings

Kari Me
www.kari-me.co.uk

Tricotti
www.birthandbaby.com

Wilkinet
www.freerangekids.co.uk

Baby Food

DIY

Make your own from organic fruit and
vegetables. Get them delivered fresh to
your door with a box scheme. To find a
box scheme go to:
www.vegboxschemes.co.uk

Ready made from organic ingredients

Babylicious
www.babylicious.co.uk

Babynat
www.goodnessdirect.co.uk

Ulula
www.ulula.co.uk

Nanny's Goat Milk Infant Nutrition
www.goodnessdirect.co.uk

Truly Scrumptious
www.bathorganicbabyfood.com

Fresh Daisy Baby Foods
www.daisyfoods.com

Peter Rabbit Organics
www.peterrabbitorganics.com

Ella's Kitchen
www.ellaskitchen.co.uk

Organix
www.organix.com

Hipp Organic
www.hipp.co.uk

Plum Baby
www.plum-baby.co.uk

Index